TO THE HEART OF THE CITY

D0581030

£1

TO THE HEART OF
THE CITY

The story of the London City Mission

Phyllis Thompson

HODDER AND STOUGHTON
LONDON   SYDNEY   AUCKLAND   TORONTO

Acknowledgments

I acknowledge with gratitude the help I received from Miss Stephanie Wright in research, Miss Carolyn Armitage and colleagues at Hodder and Stoughton in editing, Miss M Robertson in typing the manuscript and especially from all those to whom I turned for information in the London City Mission itself. Their ready co-operation made by task both congenial and inspiring.

British Library Cataloguing in Publication Data

Thompson, Phyllis, *1906*
  To the heart of the city: the story of the
  London City Mission.——(Hodder Christian
  paperbacks)
  1. London City Mission
  I. Title
  266'.022'09421   BV2865

ISBN 0 340 34727 6

Hodder and Stoughton Editorial Office: 47 Bedford Square, London WC1B 3DP

Contents

Prologue

The telephone bell rang rather late that summer evening in 1984, and as I lifted the receiver I wondered if I'd be clamping it back hard once I heard the voice at the other end of the line.

'Hello,' I said guardedly, giving my number but no name. One gets cautious about evening phone calls in the inner city. But my face relaxed into a smile as I heard, not the thick voice of an unknown man, but a woman's voice saying,

'Is that you, Phyllis? This is Jackie.'

'Jackie! How lovely to hear you again,' and I settled down for a chat. We had not been in touch since she moved out of the flat opposite, and deserting north London emigrated south of the river. Now it appeared she had moved again, and got married into the bargain. 'We've got a quaint little cottage, full of character. In Kent. I still commute to London every day, but it's good to get back here in the evening, to the trees and the lanes ...

'And how are you?' Jackie continued. 'Still writing?'

I admitted that I was.

'What's it about this time?'

'The London City Mission,' I replied, then was conscious of my brow wrinkling with perplexity as Jackie said,

'Oh, how interesting. I see it every day.'

'See it every day?' Whatever did she mean? How could she possibly see a hundred men scattered about the metropolis, traipsing up and down high-rise flats, mingling with the crowds on Tower Hill, going from door to door in new housing estates, visiting hospitals, bus depots, police stations, railways, ships in the docks, sitting alongside down-and-outs in parks, talking to drug addicts in Piccadilly ...? And even if she could see the men themselves, how could she see the driving force, the sense of mission, the inescapable conviction that this apparently desultory activity was a matter of life and death, that they had been entrusted with a message to Everyman which demanded their utmost skill and dedication to proclaim?

How could anybody *see* the London City Mission?

'Yes, I see it from the train. It's near Tower Bridge, isn't it? An impressive-looking place, with London City Mission in big letters on it. I've often wondered what it was.'

'Oh, that!' I gave a little gasp of comprehension. She was talking about a building! 'You mean the Mission head-quarters? There's quite a history attached to it.' I remembered being told that a bombed church site on Tower Bridge Road had been bought in the 1960s, with the aim of building a new headquarters there, but that planning restrictions, industrial delays and soaring prices had put the project in jeopardy. It was at this point that one of the largest legacies ever received by the Mission became available, thus solving the financial problem.

'Yes, it is quite a striking looking place,' I agreed. 'Very nice and hospitable inside, too.' I knew that from experience. The secretarial staff always seemed to find time to make me a cup of coffee, no matter at how awkward an hour I happened to arrive. 'But of course, it's the history of the Mission, and the men themselves that I'm writing about – their experiences, the situations they encounter, the lives they see changed, that sort of thing . . .'

The telephone conversation drew to a close. Jackie and I agreed that we must meet for lunch at the Barbican one day, and rang off. And my mind wandered back to a building – not a building of bricks and mortar, steel and concrete, but an invisible building of living stones, dug out of the quarries and dark, deep mines of London city, by men who had chiselled their way in to find them, slowly and doggedly, over the past 150 years.

Chapter One

FOUNDER OF MISSIONS

When David Nasmith settled in a four-roomed cottage by a canal in the East End of London for the purpose of founding a mission to the metropolis, he was not embarking on such a hare-brained scheme as might have appeared. He had had a lot of experience. Clubs and associations, missions and societies were in his blood. So many of them could claim him as founder that it is doubtful whether, at the age of thirty-six, he could have kept an accurate record of them all. As a founder of missions, it would be hard to find his equal.

It all began when he was employed as an accountant to a manufacturer, and saw an advertisement in a Glasgow newspaper:

'Clerk wanted. A person acquainted with books and accounts to act as assistant secretary to the religious societies connected with the Institution Room, 59, Glassfort Street, Glasgow ...'

Applying for the job, he learned that no fewer than twenty-three societies had agreed to conserve their expenditure by employing one man to do the office work for the lot of them. It would be his duty to call their meetings, record their minutes, keep their accounts and generally look after their several affairs. The salary offered was £60 per annum – not a munificent sum, even in 1820, but he accepted it with alacrity all the same. 'To promote the objects of such institutions has been the delightful and interesting employment of my leisure hours for the space of ten years,' he wrote, and gave the names of half-a-dozen well-known clergymen and philanthropists to whom application would be made for reference.

He obtained the job, and not only managed to fulfil his duties to everyone's satisfaction, but in the next three years formed a number of Young Men's Societies for Religious Improvement on his own account. Nor was he content to stop with religious improvement for his members. They must reach out to others more needy than themselves – to the poor in the back streets, to the slum-dwellers huddled in dingy alleys and filthy courtyards that lay around the docks, bereft of all opportunity to improve themselves.

But since most of the members of his young men's societies were working for their living, and had little time to spend in going to the slums, the obvious solution was to form a society to employ suitable men to do it.

So it came about that on the first day of January, 1826, the Glasgow City Mission was formed.

This was something new. A Mission of laymen, not trained in university or theological colleges, but able to proclaim clearly the facts of the Gospel in everyday language. What the slum-dwellers of Glasgow needed was not a gentleman with academic qualifications, but someone who could speak to them on their own level, who because of his own personal experience could tell them what it meant to have peace with God, and how to obtain it. Someone who would go to them where they lived, meet them on their own ground, sit to listen as well as to talk, and then to explain, in words they could understand, the message that was proclaimed from the pulpits of the churches into which the slum-dwellers never went. As much as the tribes of Africa, they needed a missionary.

Nasmith's vision and enthusiasm inspired others. Six young men undertook to raise the money to support one worker, and the inaugural meeting was held to launch the new society.

By the end of the year there were eight men, supported by voluntary contributions, going steadily from door to door in the poorer parts of Glasgow. By the end of the second year the number had risen to thirteen, and the Mission was proving such a success that David Nasmith wrote an account of it and sent copies far and wide, to churches not only in Scotland, England and Ireland, but to France and other countries on the continent of Europe, and to Asia, Africa and America as well. Surely this method of reaching the poor in the cities could be used elsewhere?

The enterprising young secretary to the twenty-three religious societies in Glasgow received some encouraging responses to his open letter. He was invited to Dublin, to start a city mission there. Relinquishing his present appointment he went, and eighteen months after arriving he could report that thirteen or fourteen men were now employed in missionary work in the city. He refused, however, to settle in Dublin as general secretary to the newly-formed Mission.

> I considered it to be my duty to decline upon two grounds, first, because the business is so complicated that I cannot, with safety to my health, undertake the responsibility of discharging all the duties of the office; and secondly, because I may be eminently more useful to the cause of God by going to other cities, towns and villages in Ireland, for the purpose of establishing kindred institutions, than by remaining at any one place.

In that one sentence he unconsciously summed up his own destined course, determined for him by his weakness as well as by his strength.

From Ireland he went to America, taking his wife and child with him. The sea voyage took over a month, and three weeks after arriving in New York he wrote to a friend to announce on Monday evening, September 20th, the founding of the New York City Mission. The full support of three missionaries had been guaranteed more or less on the spot. But that was only a start. By the end of 1831 he had visited over 120 cities and towns in America and Canada and had founded sixteen city missions, as well as a host of other societies: young men's societies, matrons' societies, associations on behalf of coloured people, societies on behalf of the poor generally. He did not stay long anywhere. Having achieved his object of founding associations and missions, he had left the organising and establishing of the work to others.

The success of this meteoric tour was not achieved painlessly. He had his full share of perplexities, humiliations, hardships and privations, and his wife, perhaps, had even more, for she spent most of her time in a boarding-house in New York, with their child, while he was away. It was largely on her account that he decided to establish her again in a home of her own.

'I found it was becoming necessary for the health and comfort of Mrs. Nasmith that I should settle somewhere,' he wrote to his parents, 'and seeking an extensive sphere of action, gave her the choice of New York, Paris, or London. She chose the latter.'

In such simple, unsensational ways are man's paths directed.

David Nasmith's wife chose London, confirming a deepening conviction in his own heart that it was the place to which he should go. It would have been much more congenial to have remained in America, which was experiencing the solemn thrills of spiritual revival, largely through the preaching of the famous revivalist, Charles G. Finney. Thousands were being awakened to their need of a change of heart before it was too late, among them numbers of undergraduates, and Nasmith took advantage of the opportunities given to address them, almost invariably on the subject of city missions. He wrote,

'I might have had many situations in this country, had I thought it my duty to settle here, that would have yielded a very comfortable living; but believing that, under God, I may be more useful in London than in any other city, I propose going there.'

So to London he eventually came. He passed through various difficulties before arriving, including the failure of an ambitious scheme to establish a centre for religious and philanthropic societies in Glasgow, which landed him heavily in debt. Had it not been for the moral and financial support of a group of friends in Dublin, he might never have settled in England's capital at all: although a visit to France had resulted in the formation of city missions in both Paris and Havre, he met with very little encouragement to found one in London. It might work, he was told, if linked either with the Anglican church or the nonconformists, but not if he expected it to be connected with both. The gap between the two was too wide.

> I very much fear, that in the present circumstances of the church, you will find yourself repelled at every step in any plan which contemplates the co-operation of different denominations. In the first place, you must secure the consent of the bishop, or you will not get the clergy to act, and without the clergy you will find it hard to move the lay members of the Establishment. In the second place, there is a wide gulf just now between Dissenters and the Establishment... Under these circumstances I know not what course you can take, except to choose between the Dissenters and the Establishment.

So wrote an eminent churchman, and so said the Dissenters. On that point, at any rate, they were agreed.

It was in the face of such discouragements that Nasmith, financially impoverished, took possession of a small terraced house by the canal at Hoxton in late March, 1835, and two months later, on May 16th, formed the London City Mission.

Anything simpler and less spectacular than that ceremony could scarcely be imagined. Nasmith and two friends, both laymen, knelt together in prayer, then, in Nasmith's own words,

> We there formed the London City Mission, adopted our constitution, assigned offices to each other, and after laying the infant Mission before the Lord, desiring that he would nurse and bless it and make it a blessing to tens of

thousands, we adjourned. For some months after this we met, on an average, three times a week at six o'clock in the morning, for prayer and business.

The business to which they attended, Nasmith in particular, was largely concerned with interviews and writing letters to urge on people the need and the opportunity of establishing a city mission in London. The need had already been forcibly brought home to the general public by the publication in *The Times* of a letter to the Bishop of London. The writer, himself a prominent churchman, had drawn attention to the hundreds of thousands of people in the rat-ridden, crumbling old buildings lying behind the streets of the wealthy in his Lordship's diocese. There was something unspeakably painful, he said, to realise that this mass of immortal beings, living so close to themselves, were without God and without hope. He went on to enumerate, in the language of the day, the various categories into which they fell.

500,000 Sabbath-breakers, at the very least, in total neglect of the restraints of religion, communicate the plague of ungodliness to all around them. 10,000 of these are devoted to play; above 20,000 are addicted to beggary, 30,000 are living by theft and fraud; 32,000 are in the course of the year picked up drunk in the streets; about 100,000 are habitual gin drinkers, and 100,000 or more have yielded themselves to systematic and abandoned profligacy.

Nasmith's arrival in London was opportune, for it coincided not only with the appearance of this letter, but with a general awakening of the social conscience. In spite of gloomy prognostications, once the step of founding it had been taken, the London City Mission soon gained wide-spread support. When Thomas E. Buxton, M.P., prominent in pleading for the emancipation of the slave, agreed to act as treasurer, public confidence was assured and contributions started flowing in. A sturdy, reliable working-class man had already been appointed as the first missionary, and was followed by a number of others. By December so much interest had been aroused, and so many favourable reports of the work of the missionaries received, that a public inaugural meeting was held in a large hall in central London, which lasted for five hours and attracted such crowds that many people had to be turned away. The London City Mission, with its revolutionary methods of employing lay workers on an interdenominational basis, had introduced a new element into nineteenth-century evangelism in Great Britain, and those who rejected the idea were forced to take note.

Not that all went smoothly. The Bishop of London was opposed to the whole project, making it very difficult for Anglican clergymen in his diocese to support it. And there were problems in the Mission's administration which no one had anticipated, but which threatened a severe set-back.

Strangely enough, the cause of the trouble was Nasmith himself.

The Mission now had its headquarters in Red Lion Square, Holborn, and in his position of honorary secretary, Nasmith's propensity for forming associations re-asserted itself. The committee observed with some surprise that a society for the formation of City and Town Missions throughout the whole British Empire had been started in the L.C.M. headquarters. Surprise developed into consternation when, a short time later, a Monthly Tract Society was added. Then a Young Men's Association. Then a British and Foreign Young Men's Association. Then a Reading Room. Then an Adult School Society.

Protests, mild at first, but increasing in vehemence, were made to Nasmith. It was pointed out that the business associated with the London City Mission, still in its infancy, was more than sufficient to occupy his attention. Donations were already coming in more slowly. Furthermore, church-men sympathetic to the movement were complaining that too many of the missionaries employed were nonconform-

ists, insisting that there should be a balancing number of
laymen from the Church of England. Instead of dissipating
his energies by forming new societies, should he not be
endeavouring to rectify this imbalance, especially since the
main financial support for the L.C.M. was coming from the
Anglicans?

Nasmith was unmoved by these arguments. Denomina-
tional preferences meant nothing to him and he refused to be
affected by them. As for the new societies, they were
designed for the furtherance of God's Kingdom just as much
as was the London City Mission, and he considered it his
duty to found them in the same way. He was very gracious
about it, but quite adamant.

Then, quite unwittingly, he brought things to a head by
forming yet another society – this time a rescue mission for
prostitutes called the Female Friend Society. Its premises
adjoined the L.C.M. offices – and were connected to them by
a door for convenience of administration!

The committee was horrified. 'This indelicate and
imprudent action' one of them called it, and one after
another the most important members resigned. Public
interest, already diminishing, was undermined, and eventually Nasmith realised that if the Mission were to continue
he must be the one to resign. To his great credit and his
personal grief, he did so. The few remaining members of the
committee demurred, but it was obviously the best thing for
the Mission to accept it. At a committee meeting held on
March 17th, 1837, it was resolved,

That the thanks of the managers be given to Mr. David
Nasmith, the founder and gratuitous secretary of this
Society, for his unwearied devotion to its interests; that
the managers cannot but deeply lament the occurrence of
any circumstances rendering his resignation, in his
opinion, advisable; and that it is with pain they lose the
services of one who, from his great experience and
unceasing assiduity, was an invaluable coadjutor in this
great work.

So ended David Nasmith's connection with the Mission he had founded less than two years before. It was not the end of his enthusiasm for founding societies, however. Up to the time of his sudden death in December, 1839, he was travelling constantly for that purpose, his zeal for city missions in particular being undiminished.

Some of them, it is true, were small and petered out.

Some were eventually absorbed into other associations.

But some were still going strong 150 years later.

The effects of Nasmith's vision for lay workers in the cities are to be found in every continent, for city missions exist which were either founded by him or inspired by his methods. The London City Mission has always claimed him as its founder, and honoured his memory.

Back in 1837, however, it would almost certainly have died out had he not left it. His gift was to inspire, not to administrate. Once he had resigned and the committee was free to act, friends and supporters returned, balance was restored, and the Female Friend Society discreetly moved to flourish in White Lion Street, Pentonville, leaving the L.C.M. in sole possession of the offices in Red Lion Square.

Chapter Two

THE FIRST MISSIONARIES

In the same year that young Charles Dickens, seeking material for his books, was investigating slum conditions in the neighbourhood of Spitalfields, the London City Mission sent their first worker, Lindsay Burfoot, to start visiting from door to door there. He had been chosen from among some fifty other applicants, and having successfully passed the set examination, had been instructed to visit all the inhabitants in a given area, 'to bring them to acquaintance of salvation through our Lord Jesus Christ, and do them good by every means in your power'.

With no experience other than voluntary evangelistic work done in his spare time, and no theological training beyond what he had obtained by his own efforts, he set off for the filthy alleys and stinking courtyards with their pimps and prostitutes, burglars and thieves, the Fagins and the Bill Sykeses so vividly depicted in *Oliver Twist*. He carried a Bible with him, and a pocketful of tracts, and that was all. If he didn't know enough to leave his watch at home, and secrete his handkerchief and his money so deep in his clothing that even he himself had difficulty in extracting them, he soon learned to do so. The children were too well trained when it came to snatching handkerchiefs or deftly inserting little hands into coat pockets, for him to take any chances with his few possessions.

The Mission paid him £1 a week for his services. That didn't go very far, even in those days, but when he saw the expression of despair on the faces of men and women who had nothing left to pawn he felt himself to be well off indeed. As he threaded his way along the deep, miry gullies between the dilapidated old houses, poverty and squalor assailed his eyes, bad smells his nostrils, obscene language his ears. He was a sturdy man, accustomed to roughing it, but as he emerged from hovels where he had seen alcoholics, or fever-stricken children lying in their own vomit and excrement, there were times when he was unable to control the nausea that overcame him. There were days when he returned home with a splitting headache, after seven or eight hours on his feet trying to keep mentally and spiritually alert enough to parry with good humour the insults and sneers hurled at him. And there were nights when his nerve seemed near to breaking, as he faced going again into the courtyards where he'd been shouted at, shoved, even knocked over, sur-rounded by jeering drunks and screaming women. He looked longingly at some of the more respectable streets and alleys which he passed on his way to the particular slum area allotted to him, and one day asked the young vicar of the parish, who superintended his work, if he could include them in his visitation, 'just for a bit of a change'. But his request was refused.

'Better stick to the rules,' he was told, sympathetically enough. 'The idea is for you to get really well known there in Artillery Ground and Norton Folgate. They won't listen to you till they know you, but when they do you'll have your chance. It's bound to be hard at the start.'

The vicar, as it happened, was having his own problems. An ardent supporter of the pioneering London City Mission, he was acting as its honorary secretary when he received a letter from his bishop telling him in politely clerical language to give it up. After an acute conflict between apparently divergent loyalties, he reluctantly decided to resign from the L.C.M., and wrote to tell the bishop that he had done so. There was, however, a sting in the tail of the respectful letter, as the bishop realised when he read,

'I must add, especially as there is considerable excitement in the matter, that the responsibility of the act must be Your Lordship's, and not my own.'

This was awkward. The rapidly growing Mission, now with some twenty missionaries, was gaining widespread interest and approbation. The Bishop of London would be put in an unfavourable light if it became known to what an extent he was opposing it. After some weeks he wrote acknowledging the vicar's letter, but added,

'I must decline any responsibility being cast on me, as this rests entirely with yourself.'

That was all the vicar needed to know. He promptly withdrew his resignation from the L.C.M., asking to be reinstated, and wrote to inform the bishop of what he had done since, as he explained, it seemed unreasonable for anyone in authority not to accept responsibility for an order given and acted upon. That round undoubtedly went to the vicar, and it is to the bishop's credit that so far from holding it against him, he went out of his way to show personal kindness to the strong-minded young incumbent. It took him much longer to acknowledge the value of the L.C.M. itself.

As for Lindsay Burfoot, he stuck it out in Spitalfields. Not all were able to do so. Of the first ten men appointed by the Mission, seven were out of the work within two years, either from illnesses caught in the fever-ridden rooms, debilities brought about by physical assaults, or sheer discouragement in the face of daily hostility. But those who were strong enough physically, nervously and spiritually to endure, began to win their way.

With some, however, it was slow going. There was the eager young fellow, for instance, who was taken along to Paradise Court. His superintendent told him that it was the worst place in the district, advised him to start visiting on the top floor and work down, and then left him to get on with it. He started his visitation with bright hopes.

In the first room were six grimy-looking men, cobblers, and as soon as they knew he had come to talk about God asserted that there wasn't one, and ordered him out. Entering the next room he saw, to his horror, the body of a dead child on the floor, while on the bed lay a woman and a little girl, both flushed with high fever. The father of the family, he was told, had gone out to get some money by singing on the streets, but would be back soon, as he was very cut up by Bobby dying in the night. The inexperienced young missionary, stunned and bewildered, not knowing what else to do, read a few verses from his pocket Bible, prayed and went to the next room. Here an old woman was frying some fish so putrid that the smell made him reel. All she wanted was money – she thought he might be the Relieving Officer. Money was all the women wanted who lived in the next room, too. When he mentioned the true riches and produced his Bible they shut the door in his face. And so it went on, till by evening he went home feeling so despondent that he decided he'd take the next day off to get over it.

The day after that was Sunday, so he went again, and this time there was one bright encounter, for he met the widow with the teapot. Hearing a few cracked voices singing,

> Come ye that love the Lord
> And let your joys be known...

he went along to investigate. Entering the room he found four old women perched on the edge of a bed, and Widow Peters sitting facing them, with a Bible in her hand. The widow was in her seventies, and she told him he was the answer to her prayers, because when she had heard of missionaries going to other slum areas to tell the people about Jesus and the way to heaven, she had started to plead with God to send one to Paradise Court. The teapot, he soon discovered, contained her panacea for most human ills and emotional upsets. The people in Paradise Court were used to seeing her hurrying along with an apron carefully covering it to keep it hot, to visit some young woman who had just had a baby, or a sobbing mother who had just lost one, or a hysterical wife who'd just had a row with her husband, or an old man reported to be dying. 'Here, dear, a nice cup of tea will do you good,' and somehow, as most people agreed, it did. The young missionary found from time to time that it did him good, too, though a talk and a prayer with the old widow proved even better. The two of them were allies, and in all that happened later he acknowledged her support.

The young missionary visited in Paradise Court for several months with little apparent effect, except that he noticed people subdued their bad language when he was around. On one occasion, coming on a fight where two furious women were being egged on by a crowd to scratch and pull each other's hair out, his look of stern disapproval had almost miraculously melted the onlookers away, leaving the two combatants, on seeing him, to disappear shame-facedly behind their respective doors. It occurred to him, as he walked on, that it would have taken half-a-dozen policemen to accomplish what his own silent presence had apparently achieved. He felt he must be making some headway after all.

Opportunities come in unexpected ways, and pass so quickly that if not grasped at the time they are lost for ever.

The young man's great opportunity came when the widow ran up to him one day and explained breathlessly that a woman was ill of the black fever: she had to be taken to the infirmary, but no one was willing to go near enough to put her on the stretcher. Everyone was too frightened of catching the plague. So the young missionary went along, picked up the patient, carried her out of her room, down the stairs and on to the stretcher, and accompanied her to the workhouse. It all happened so naturally and quickly that he would probably have thought no more about it had it not been for the effect it had on the people in Paradise Court. When he reappeared, an appreciative murmur greeted him, very different from the sneers and the indifference to which he was becoming accustomed. He was suddenly in their favour, he realised, and was quick to take advantage of it. Springing onto a fishmonger's barrow he called out,

'The plague! The plague! Help me to drive out the plague!' They stared at him speechless for once, and he continued.

'We must get rid of it, or it will get rid of us. The plague is here, and you've asked for it. Oh, yes, you have! I'm going to speak to you plainly, as a good friend should. How have you asked for it? Because you haven't got enough air and water. The plague hates air and water. You sleep together six or seven in a room and never open the window. The air gets poisoned, and you breathe it in, and the fever weakens you, and the fever wins. Another thing. You don't use enough water. The fever thrives on dirt. Fight it! Wash your clothes, wash your children. Wage war on the fever with water! Wash down the streets ...

'Why not wash down the streets? You're the ones who live in them, aren't you? If every one of you threw a bucket of water on the cobbles, think how that would clean things up. Then there are your water butts. They need cleaning out. Clean them out, put fresh water in when the water's turned on. Turn the plague out!

'Another thing – scrub your rooms and the stairs, then whitewash them...

'Leave that to the landlords, you say? You'll be dead before they do anything! Agreed? Well, then, do it yourselves. A bucket of whitewash costs no more than a pint of beer. If you'll do it, I'll speak to the Parochial Officer of Health, and see if he'll refund you the money.

'Out with the plague! Fight the fever yourselves. It's very fond of drunkards with their bad breath and their weakened bodies.' He was on delicate ground now, and he knew it. The gin palaces carried on a thriving trade in Paradise Court, especially at the weekends when the men who had found work picked up their wages.

'If you want to drive out the plague, you need to do three things. One – more fresh air and water. Two – every room whitewashed. Three – a sober Saturday night!

'I'll say it again,' he shouted. 'A sober Saturday night! Promise you'll do those three things, and I'll see what help I can get for you.'

Just at this point Drunken Sammy, the local clown, appeared on the scene. He was usually greeted with laughs and shouts as he gesticulated and tumbled around, but this time the crowd, quietened by their fear of the plague and the missionary's unusual note of authority, looked at him without a smile.

'There's that fool of a Sammy!' snorted one of the women irritably. The missionary, quick to grasp an advantage, saw a simple way of dealing with a troublesome customer.

'Look after that poor man, will you?' he said, turning to the woman. 'Don't let him out of his room till I come again tomorrow afternoon. A sober Saturday night for Sammy!'

'We'll do that!' Two or three women, who lived in the same house, came forward, grabbed Drunken Sammy by the arms, and bundled him indoors. 'A sober Saturday night is just what he needs. We'll see he has it.'

The missionary walked away, smiling to himself. Drunken Sammy would have resisted arrest by the police with spirit, and Paradise Court would have been on his side to a man, demanding human rights, but no one uttered a word on his behalf now as he went, unprotesting, to his imprisonment. He remained there all Saturday, and Sunday as well, and by that time he was sober. He had had no option. His captors had shown no mercy, in spite of his shouts and door bangings.

Drunken Sammy did not like being sober. It made him afraid. Memories had a way of welling up from the past and pointing an accusing finger at him, reminding him that his sins were still there, however feverishly he tried to avoid facing them. They were facing him now. Sunday morning came, and with it the distant sound of church bells chiming, adding to his uneasiness with their reminder that there was a God to be faced at the end.

The day dragged on, and Sammy was sinking deeper and deeper into gloom, when he heard voices outside, the door was unlocked, and who should enter but the widow with her teapot.

'I thought you might maybe like a cup of tea, Sammy,' she said. 'It'll make you feel better. The milk's in with it, and here's some sugar,' producing a few knobs from her pocket. 'Now let's find a cup. That mug'll do. That's right, drink it up. There's more in the pot. You'd do a lot better, Sammy, if you drank more tea and less gin,' and as Sammy sucked in the tea she went on chatting, till she saw his face crumpling up, then his hands going to clutch his head. He looked as though he was about to cry. Then he started talking about his wife.

'I know I must have killed her,' he groaned. 'I beat her so hard, she never got over it.' The widow nodded. All Paradise Court knew about the affair, and how he'd come up for trial, and the jury had pronounced him 'not guilty' but the judge had given him such a dressing-down, he'd never forgotten it. He'd drunk more than ever after that, for 'he's got something on his mind,' the inhabitants of Paradise Court said understandingly. They didn't say what it was. Everybody knew. They laughed uproariously when he appeared with his tumblings and his clownings, joining with him in the effort to forget what he couldn't put right.

But the widow did not laugh.

'Yes, Sammy, you're a poor sinner,' she agreed. 'But the blessed Lord died for you. He was punished for your sin. Now that you feel how bad you are, you must not look to yourself, you must look to Jesus. Look to the dear Jesus. One drop of His precious blood is enough to make you clean and happy. Let me pray for you, Sammy.'

She did not know that two men were standing outside the door, listening to her. The missionary had not been idle since leaving Paradise Court. He had made several calls which had resulted in the Parochial Officer of Health agreeing to accompany him to the slum to see conditions for himself, and it was they who had just arrived. The Officer of Health had lifted his eyebrows in surprise to find the Court well washed with buckets of water, and sniffed inquisitively at the smell of lime and had enquired what it was all about as he saw signs of whitewash being applied in doorways. The missionary, very relieved to see that the promises made were being kept, explained what had happened.

'You are welcome to take over my duties for the whole parish!' said the medical man drily. 'The solution to the sanitary problem is to influence these people to act for themselves, and you've done it. I'll see to it that a report goes in that will result in better drainage and a better water supply here.' And as he stood in the narrow passage and heard the widow praying with the drunkard, it was evident that he was touched. 'Send the old woman to me tomorrow and I'll give her some medicine that will help cure that man's craving for drink,' he said. 'I'd like to help you in your work of reformation...'

As they were leaving the Court they met a group of scavengers. 'You've knocked off early today,' said the missionary, recognising one of them.

'No, we ain't knocked off yet,' was the reply. 'We're a-goin' to clean out this place. I didn't wash the dust down with gin last night, so I've got some money to give these chaps to help, and the carts are comin...'

The Parochial Health Officer went on his way with wonder. He'd never known anything like it before. He saw to it that the drainage system and the water supply were improved, and that the local authorities knew about that young fellow belonging to the City Mission. He was likely to be helpful.

The matter did not stop there. The story of the widow with the teapot reached the ears of the daughter of a naval officer, who asked the missionary to send the old lady to see her.

'I'd like to pay her rent from now on,' she said. 'And give her some warm clothing. Through her I may be able to help you in the work you are doing.'

If the people of Paradise Court weren't so sure about the Lord they neither saw nor heard, they couldn't deny the evidence of a kind heart somewhere that was touched by human need. The sweep who lived at the corner said, 'Who would have believed it? Here we are, forsaken by God and man, and now...' As other tangible evidences of kindness began to filter through from an unseen source, there was an easing of the attitude of angry despair the young missionary had encountered at the first.

The man who had gone to sing on the streets because he had no money on the night his little Bobby died, had sneered contemptuously at the suggestion of prayer, but when food and clothing arrived for his other child, his attitude changed. When a young labourer who couldn't find work was presented with a pickaxe to enable him to get a job, and when several women were loaned money to set up as street traders, and people who were sick received gifts of invalid food, Paradise Court began to think there might be someone who cared after all. They were willing to concede that the young missionary and the widow with her teapot had a point when they talked about God loving them. Some of them began to ask questions, read the tracts that pointed out the dangers of drunkenness and the power they could receive from Christ to overcome the craving – and even dropped in at the widow's room when the missionary was preaching there, so that eventually he had to rent a room especially for that purpose. It created quite a stir when it was learned that Drunken Sammy had given up the drink, signed the pledge, and was going to chapel every Sunday, and that two of the women who lived in the same house were going as well.

The fishmonger's wedding set a new fashion, too. 'Young Tom from Whitechapel wants to take our Bess as his lawful wedded wife,' the missionary was told, then consulted as to the best way of going about it. It was arranged that the wedding should take place in church, with the banns being read for three Sundays before the event in the presence of those concerned, sitting awkwardly in the free pews. The buzz and hum of excitement in Paradise Court when the happy pair returned from the ceremony for the wedding breakfast (prepared by the widow with the teapot) was quite different from the usual sounds heard there. And the missionary, invited to say something, read with a voice somehow deeper than usual because charged with emotion, the record of a wedding in Cana in Galilee, where Jesus was one of the guests.

After that there were other weddings in Paradise Court – rather quieter than the fishmonger's, as the parties concerned had been living together on and off for years, so they didn't want to make a big fuss about it. But somehow they were beginning to feel uncomfortable, going on the way they were, and in a rather embarrassed manner sought a quiet talk with the missionary to see if he could help them to straighten things out. He became quite accustomed to acting as 'father' to the bride. On one morning alone he gave away three 'brides', while the Rector, knowing their poverty, remitted the fees. He had won his way into Paradise Court. The people were willing to listen to him now, and sneered no more when he produced his Bible and spoke of hell and judgment on the one hand, and heaven and forgiveness on the other.

He pulled no punches in his preaching, and nor did any of the others. They were tough, those early City Missionaries, with their warnings of sin's consequences, and their stern denunciations of godlessness. They had to be. The people they went to were hardened. The dock workers and coal heavers and street women around the Port of London, the pig-feeders of Fifty Acres in Kensington, the men and women in the filthy streets of Billingsgate and Smithfield, the denizens of the 'Poverty Squares' of the West End, the millions of the lower classes whose misery was pushed out of sight and out of mind until their cry reached up to heaven, were hard and bitter and crafty. They had known no other way to survive. The missionaries who went to them had to be tough, but they were cheerful, too, quick with the reconciling word, smart with repartee, and ready with a helping hand, as many an old woman discovered. So they made their way into the dens and rookeries where the thieves had their secret escape routes along roofs, into the miserable tenements where one-room families slept together on one sagging bed, and into the workhouses where dreary lives ended and equally dreary lives began.

Lives like those of Charlie Bin and Mary Bundle, for instance. They were so called because Charlie had been found as a baby in a dustbin, and Mary in a bundle of rags at the workhouse door. At the age of six Charlie was 'adopted' by a chimney sweep, who soon had the little lad climbing up the dark, soot-laden labyrinthine tunnels that wound from fireplace to chimney stack. He was encouraged by lighted paper or pins stuck into his feet when he evinced too early a desire to come down. Mary, aged eight, was taken by a respectable-looking woman who applied for a girl to be trained in needlework, who received a sum of money for looking after her. The money, not the child, was the attraction. The maternal instincts of the pauper women who had been deputed to look after the orphans were not strongly developed, but even they were horrified at what they saw a few months later, when Mary ran in one morning at the workhouse door, having managed to escape from her mistress and come 'home'. She was so thin and emaciated that they scarcely recognised her, and when they saw her body, covered with bruises and weals, they reported it to the authorities. It was with some satisfaction that the missionary, who took a personal interest in the little orphans, learnt that Mary's mistress had been arrested and sentenced at the Central Criminal Court to two years' imprisonment with hard labour. As he knew, too many of those who perpetrated such cruelties were allowed to get away with it. The children who survived grew up morose and brutalised, to add another generation to the line of destitute idlers and criminals from which most of them had sprung.

Charlie and Mary both died quite young, as it happened: Charlie of 'soot cancer', Mary after a short and sudden illness which her weakened constitution could not fight. They waited very patiently for the end, smiling weakly at the missionary when he visited them, nodding confidently as he talked to them of the 'happy land, far far away' in which Jesus was preparing a place for them. They weren't sorry to be going.

What happened to Thomas Miller at the end, nobody knows. He was first arrested at the age of eight, for stealing some boxes, and sentenced to a month's imprisonment and a whipping. He was one of the unlucky ones, his fellow juvenile thieves agreed, for a short time later he was caught again, this time robbing a till. He got three months for that. He was no sooner out than he was in prison again, this time for three years. By the age of twelve he stood 4 feet 2.inches

Chapter Three

THE CRY OF THE CHILDREN

A woman had tried to murder her three children by throwing them into the Regent's Canal, then to commit suicide by throwing herself in after them. Had it not been that the cries of the children were heard by a young tailor who happened to be crossing a nearby bridge at the time and rushed to rescue them, they would all have been drowned.

Newspaper reporters, of course, followed the story up to the time of the trial at the Central Criminal Court. Largely on the strength of evidence supplied by a London City missionary, the jury returned a verdict that the prisoner had attempted murder and suicide while in a state of insanity, brought on by the cruel treatment of her husband. The judge sentenced her to detention, as insane, during Her Majesty's pleasure. And that, as far as the reporters were concerned, was the end of the story.

What they did not know was that the City missionary, whose efforts to bring the husband to his senses before the trial had failed because the man was never sober, decided to try again. It took some courage to go and confront him, for he was a huge fellow and so strong that he could lift the corner of a bus and hold it while a wheel was being changed – a job he was often called upon to perform as a worker in the omnibus yard. His wife had been terrified of him when he got in a drunken rage. 'Oh, he does hit so hard!' she had told the missionary. 'He beat me last week and the swelling hasn't gone down yet. My poor little girls are almost frightened to death.' And now she was in prison, the children without their mother, and the man . . . ?

The missionary was indignant. The man who was

responsible for it all had got off scot-free. He needed to be confronted with his crime, and the missionary knew that if he didn't do it, nobody else would. So on the Sunday morning after the trial he went again to the house where the family had lived, found the door unfastened, and without so much as a knock flung it open and entered.

'Higgers, you are as bad as a murderer!' he said sternly. The man, slumped in a chair, startled by the unceremonious entry, looked up in amazement. The missionary, still burning with anger, continued,

'You swore before Almighty God that you would love and cherish that poor wife of yours, and what have you done? Your brutality drove her to try to murder your children and kill herself. You are the one who is guilty. And what has caused it? Drink! Drink! Your love of drink!'

Higgers was on his feet by now, fists clenched, ready to attack, but his accuser stood firm, looked him in the eyes and said,

'For what you have done *you* must stand trial.' He paused a moment, and then, as one invested with supreme authority, pronounced,

'You must stand before the judgement seat of Christ.'

There was silence in the room after that. It lasted but a moment or two of time, but the quality of eternity was in it. The man, his fists still clenched, retreated towards the window and the missionary knew that his words had struck home. If that had been the only message he had to deliver, he could have turned on his heel and departed. However, it was not his only message. In the hours that followed he spoke of the mercy and forgiveness offered to those who will humble themselves to accept it, speaking softly now, till the man sat down with his head in his hands, weeping as though his very soul was forcing its way up through his tears. 'God forgive me... God forgive me...'

At last, exhausted, his sobs ceased, and the missionary took a practical line.

'Now Higgers, we must see what you have to do about it,' he said. 'If you'd broken your arm, you'd want to have it mended. And if I was a doctor, you'd let me set it for you and do what I told you, wouldn't you? Well, I'm a sort of doctor, not of the body but the soul. It's your soul that needs healing. Are you willing to do what I tell you to do?'

Higgers took his time before answering. He did not know what demands might be made, or whether he would have the ability to fulfil them. But after a short pause he looked up, held out his hand, and said,

'Yes, sir, I will. And here's my fist on it.'

'Then promise me that you'll give up the drink once for all. That's the first.' Higgers nodded, slowly and thoughtfully.

'And secondly,' the missionary gave a little grin. This was going to be much easier. 'Secondly – come home with me and have some dinner!' But this time Higgers shook his head.

'Thank you sir,' he said. 'But I can't eat. My wife in prison, my little girls with their granny, afraid to come back to me, my baby in the workhouse ... I'm too wretched to eat. And I'm in no fit state to go out, looking like this.' His eyes were red and his face swollen with weeping. 'But I'll come to you about five o'clock – I promise.' And he kept his word.

So that evening the missionary and his wife entertained him to tea, then took him to a Christian Temperance Meeting where he signed the pledge never to drink intoxicating liquor again, met some reformed drunkards eager to befriend him, and went home.

A few Saturdays later he turned up at the missionary's home with a request. 'I want you to keep my savings for me,' he said. 'I've paid all my debts at the pub, and got our things out of pawn, and now I'm afraid I'll be tempted with so much money in my pocket.'

'Come in!' was the enthusiastic reply. 'I'll keep your money for you till you need it – but now we must talk over your affairs, and see how we can get you resettled with the children.' It took some time, as a good many arrangements had to be made, but eventually the three little girls were back with their father in their own home, with their granny to look after them.

To restore the mother to her family, however, seemed an

impossibility. The indeterminate sentence of detention 'at Her Majesty's pleasure' could last for years, even for a lifetime.

'We must pray about this – there's nothing else that we can do,' said the missionary, little knowing the chain of events that had already been set in motion, and how the answer would come.

It so happened that a well-known Manchester man, interested in the reformation of drunkards, had seen the newspaper report of Higgers' wife's conviction. Some time later, on visiting London, he made enquiries about Higgers, was put in touch with the missionary, heard about the change that had taken place in the man and then met him personally. He then related the case to the famous parliamentarian, Richard Cobden, who, having invited the missionary to breakfast to hear the story at first hand, brought the case before the Home Secretary. That dignitary expressed his willingness to look into the affair, and the London City missionary, accustomed to door-to-door visiting in the streets of the poor, now found himself in the library of the House of Commons, again relating the facts about Mrs. Higgers, this time to Sir George Grey.

'I'll find out what her mental condition is, and see what can be done about getting her release,' was the assurance he received at the end of the interview.

And so it came about that a week later a hansom cab clattered along the narrow street where Higgers lived, and out stepped Mrs. Higgers straight into the arms of her husband, while their little girls danced delightedly around, clamouring for attention too. What with the expressions of amazement on the part of Mrs. Higgers at the new shawl and the dress material her husband had bought for her, the wonder of the wardress who had accompanied her at the rapture of the welcome, and the general excitement of the neighbours who had come along to join in, it was some time before things quietened down sufficiently for the missionary to suggest that they knelt to thank Almighty God whose power and mercy had brought all this happiness out of sin and despair.

Some weeks later the missionary again visited the family, this time accompanied by a well-dressed, genial gentleman who, while playing with the children, chatted casually to Higgers. The conversation turned naturally to subjects relating to the conditions of working-class people, the value of benefit clubs, and such like. It gave the gentlemen a useful insight into the way working-class people lived and thought. Not until years later did the missionary divulge the fact that the visitor was none other than the famous Mr. Richard Cobden, fervent advocate of free trade, whose agitation against laws restricting the import of corn had resulted, among other things, in bread being cheaper. The London City missionary had provided a useful link between the poor and the ruling class.

It was not the only time such a thing happened, and interestingly enough, not the only time that it all started with the casual perusal of a daily paper. The first that Lord Ashley, heir to the Earl of Shaftesbury, knew about the London City Mission was through something he read in *The Times* one day in February, 1843. For years he had been worried about the waifs and strays he saw on the streets of London, and felt it his duty to improve their lot, but did not know how to set about it. The problems of poverty and destitution were far too widespread to be dealt with by one man. Something needed to be done at the grass roots, and how could he, a member of the aristocracy, ever hope to get to that level at all?

He could imagine some of the pains and privations they endured. His own childhood had been a bitterly unhappy one. Left by his parents to the mercy of servants, the lonely little fellow, heir to the great estate, had often gone hungry and cold to bed. And when, at the age of seven, he was sent away to boarding school, he lived in constant fear of making the mistakes which would bring down heartless punishment on his head, and of the older boys who were allowed to bully the younger ones unmercifully. The only comfort in his life was derived from an old family servant, Maria Millis, a simple-hearted, devout woman who really loved the child. It was she, not his mother, who had taken him on her lap, told him Bible stories, taught him to pray. He was stricken with a grief that he could share with no one when he heard that she had died, and years later the gold watch she had left him in her will was still his most precious possession. 'It was given to me by the best friend I ever had,' he often said, and never wore any other. The wide gulf between the nobility and the lower classes had been bridged in his childhood by that friendship of mutual love and respect, but how could it be bridged now?

The answer to his question, and to his frequent prayers on the subject was in sight when he read an advertisement which ran

RAGGED SCHOOLS
Field Lane Sabbath School,
65, West Street, Saffron Hill

The Teachers are desirous of laying before the public a few facts connected with this school, situated in this most wretched and demoralised locality. It was opened in 1841 for instructing (free of expense) those who, from their poverty and ragged condition, are prevented attending any other place of religious instruction. The school is under the superintendence of the District Missionary of the London City Mission, and is opened on Sunday and also on Thursday evening, when the average attendance is seventy (adults and children). The teachers are encouraged by the success which, under God, has attended their efforts, as manifested by the increased numbers, and altered conduct of some of the scholars. This appeal to the Christian public is made to afford permanency to a work of charity, commenced and supported by a few laymen, whose means are inadequate to the expenses necessarily attendant upon the enlarged state of the school. Any lady or gentleman willing to assist as teachers will be cordially welcomed. Donations and subscriptions will be thankfully received.

He did not hesitate about responding to the advertisement. His was one of the first replies received, and to the organisers' surprise it was followed shortly afterwards by a personal visit. What Lord Ashley saw there has been vividly described by Charles Dickens, who visited the place about the same time. He wrote,

> I found my first Ragged School ... pitifully struggling for life under every disadvantage. It had no means; it had no suitable rooms; it derived no power or protection from being recognized by any authority; it attracted within its walls a fluctuating swarm of faces – young in years, but youthful in nothing else – that scowled Hope out of countenance. It was held in a low-roofed den, in a sickening atmosphere, in the midst of taint, and dirt, and pestilence; with all the deadly sins let loose, howling and shrieking at the doors. Zeal did not supply the place of method and training; the teachers knew little of their office; the pupils, with an evil sharpness, found them out, got the better of them, derided them, made blasphemous answers to Scriptural questions, sang, fought, danced, robbed each other – seemed possessed by legions of devils. The place was stormed and carried, over and over again; the lights were blown out, the books strewn in the gutters, and the female scholars carried off triumphantly to their old wickedness...[1]

This was the atmosphere in which the future Earl of Shaftesbury bridged the gulf, and found friends of the same calibre as Maria Millis. The London City Mission men of those days were themselves from the working classes, but there were those among them who became his personal friends. One of them was Roger Miller, who had started a Ragged School in south London. When he was killed in a railway accident, Lord Ashley attended the funeral, and afterwards wrote in his diary,

[1] *The Life and Work of the Seventh Earl of Shaftesbury K.G.* by Edwin Hodder (Cassell & Co.) p.260

A far greater man might have gone out of the world with much less effect. All was grief on Monday at Broadwall; children and adults wept alike, and blessed the memory of poor Miller. I have known men of a hundred thousand a year depart this life and every eye as dry as a pavement. Here goes a City missionary at thirty shillings a week, and hundreds are in an agony of sorrow ... I have lost an intimate friend. We took, I may say, 'sweet counsel together'. A gap has been made in my life and occupations which will not easily be filled up.

It was his close association with such men that provided him with the authentic facts and descriptions of the circumstances of the poor which added poignancy and conviction to his speeches on their behalf in Parliament. He was already well known for his political struggles to alleviate the inhuman lot of paupers with psychiatric illnesses in the infamous lunatic asylums to which they were consigned. At the time of his introduction to the London City Mission he was still fighting to get through Parliament the Ten Hour Bill, which would restrict the exploitation of child labour in factories. Now he added to his concerns the improving of conditions for the poor in London, especially in the matter of education, which would put within their power the means of improving their own circumstances. Ragged Schools, as they were called, similar to that in Field Lane, had been started in several other areas in London; four men, a solicitor's clerk, a draper, a dealer in second-hand tools and a London City missionary had formed them into a Union. When he was approached with the request that he give it his name and his influence by becoming its President, he agreed willingly. It provided him with a further opportunity to investigate at first hand the plight of those beings on the other side of the gulf of class distinction who he felt it his duty to help. The people best able to lead him among them he soon found to be the London City missionaries. So the lives of these men, widely separated by birth and social status, were woven together like threads of a tapestry, to produce a slowly changing picture of conditions in London.

Their common faith, based on an unswerving confidence in the Bible as being God's revelation to man, and in His Son, Jesus Christ, as being the only Saviour from sin and eternal death bound them together. Lord Ashley had no room for the 'new' theology that was infiltrating the rather dead orthodoxy of the day. 'A discourse of omissions,' was the way he drily summed up a sermon he heard in a parish church one Good Friday, finding fault not so much with what the preacher said as with what he left unsaid. The missionaries he accompanied to meetings in the slums did not speak in such cultured accents as the reverend gentleman in the parish church, but what they had to say was much more to his taste. And they said it in a way that was very relevant to their listeners. He was favourably impressed with what he saw and heard.

With Thomas Jackson, for instance. Jackson had been allotted an area in Whitechapel notorious for what might be termed its illegal industries. Here were congregated the burglars and the thieves, the prostitutes and the con-men, the receivers of stolen goods and the wily disposers of them, all very industrious in their specialised departments of vice and crime. Among them were numbers of Roman Catholics from Ireland, as vociferous in defending their faith as they were faulty in adorning it. The marvel is that Thomas Jackson emerged alive from their midst when they learned that he himself had been a Roman Catholic once, but after reading the New Testament had been converted and joined the Methodists. That such a heretic should come to them preaching repentance towards God and faith in Jesus Christ, completely by-passing the virgin Mary, was an incredible impertinence, to say the least, and the Irishmen did not stop at saying the least. What indignities and abuses, blows and shoves Jackson had to endure before he was accepted into the community he did not tell, though he often said it had taken all his strength and courage, 'with the aid of constant grace' to gain an entry.

He was not without natural advantages, however. He was

tall and well built, had a broad, genial face, and a very disarming smile which even his enemies found hard to resist, and which soon won over those who had nothing against him. It did not take them long to discover that although he told them in a very forthright manner where they were wrong, he did it to their faces, not behind their backs, and that he was out to do them good, not to report them to the police. The committee member who agreed to preside at a communal tea party Jackson had organised in his district was amazed to find 300 people gathered, the poorest of the poor, with a number of burglars among them. What was even more surprising was the way Jackson gave a report for all to hear of what was going on among them.

'You will be glad to know that the young fellow I met in the cellar of the old lodging house has been praying for a new heart, and doesn't steal any more. I've got him somewhere now where he'll learn a trade.

'In the other lodging house I had a sharp talk with a roomful of rough fellows. Two or three of them are here now, and I'm glad to see them.

'One of them said he'd been in prison he forgot how many times, and I told him he must be a very clumsy fellow to have got caught so often – then I told him that Jesus Christ wanted to be his Saviour. Well, he came with eight others to the thieves' prayer meeting, and is being helped to a better life.'

He made no secret of his aim, and since his preaching and praying was followed up by practical help, they were willing to listen to him and confide to him their difficulties. They talked among themselves about what he had said, too, and it was as the result of this strange fraternising that Lord Ashley received a letter from Jackson enclosing a round robin signed by about forty thieves and burglars, asking him in the most respectful manner to meet them and give them his advice about giving up their profession.

This invitation came as the outcome of a speech he had made in Parliament on the subject of emigration. The thieves saw in emigration the one means whereby they could make a fresh start. Lord Ashley responded immediately, agreeing to meet them, and at the time appointed went to the hall in south London with Jackson.

It is doubtful whether, in the whole of London's history, a stranger gathering has ever been held. Some 350 men were there, all of them having been convicted of robbery in some form, from the smartly dressed con-men in their black coats and white neck-cloths to the unkempt, unshaven thugs of the docks. Jackson had taken the precaution of having on the doors men who were fellow criminals, who would refuse entry to anyone unable to prove he had served a prison sentence. There must be no possibility of matters that would be discussed being reported, or of anyone being arrested because of what was divulged at the meeting. Those who entered must be those whose own records would prevent them from betraying others. So there they sat, a hetero-geneous assembly of thieves, waiting for their missionary and for the aristocrat who would be accompanying him. All eyes were turned on them when they arrived, unescorted and unprotected, to walk up to the platform and take their places there.

Everything was conducted in a very orderly fashion, like a religious service. Jackson took charge, announcing a hymn which all did their best to sing in tune, then prayed, then read Luke's description of the crucifixion of Christ with the two thieves. After that he turned to Lord Ashley and read an address explaining that the purpose of the meeting was to help some of the many people who came to his home wanting to find a better way of life. Then he turned to the audience and said,

'His Lordship wants to know the particular character of the men here. You who live by burglary and more serious crimes go and sit on the right, and the others on the left.' He said it in quite a matter-of-fact way, and they responded in the same manner. When they had all settled down again there were about two hundred self-acknowledged burglars on the right, and the same number of petty thieves, shop-lifters and pick-pockets, on the left.

Then the man all had come to see rose to his feet to address them – tall, slender, immaculately dressed, with every hair in order, an aristocrat to his finger-tips. The men looked at him with respect, not unmingled with awe. He was like a being from another realm, and so must some of them have appeared to him. But he spoke quite simply, establishing a relationship with them straight away by saying that he had come at their request, not only because he felt it to be his duty, but out of regard for them. Now he wanted to hear what they had to say, and answer their questions if he could.

One after another some of the men stood up and told their stories. 'And anything more curious, more graphic, more picturesque and more touching I never heard in my life,' Lord Ashley reported later, admitting that he felt over-whelmed by the magnitude of their problems. 'How are we to live – we must either steal or die,' said one of the men, and when Jackson urged him to pray, as God could help him, Lord Ashley felt a certain sympathy with the man who replied, 'Prayer is very good, but it won't fill an empty stomach.' The spontaneous 'hear! hear!' from all over the hall showed how the others felt.

There was one man who could support Jackson's claim, however. He had a rugged story to tell of how he determined to follow Jackson's advice, give up thieving, and trust in prayer to God. He admitted that at first he had nearly starved, that in his eagerness to get work he had walked all the way to Exeter, hearing there was employment there, only to be disappointed, and had walked, barefooted by this time, all the way back. Jackson had helped him, encouraged him, and eventually he had got a job, a poorly paid one at first, but slowly his position improved until now he had a respectable situation. It had been hard going, but he stood there now as a monument to what prayer to God could achieve. There were no more arguments against prayer after that.

When the time came for the men to ask questions, these were mainly on the subject of emigration. How could they set about emigrating to Canada or Australia, what was involved, what would be required by them? Lord Ashley answered their questions as best he could, and as the meeting drew to a close one man, speaking for the others, rose and said anxiously,

'But will you ever come back to see us again?' He had talked to them as man to man, seemed to understand the web of poverty and crime that imprisoned them, this noble lord from a realm so far removed from their own – and now he was leaving! They saw him at that moment as their only life-line. 'Will you ever come back to see us again?'

'Yes,' was the firm reply. 'At any time and at any place, whenever you shall send for me.'

The murmur of gratitude and relief that followed moved him almost to tears. He must do his utmost to help these men. He must raise his voice on their behalf, reveal to others their plight, sting to action those whose privileges demanded that they should also carry responsibilities.

He took action himself. He headed a subscription list to get funds to help the emigration scheme. Less than three months later thirteen of those who had been at the meeting were on their way to a new life in Canada, and in the years that followed, hundreds more from London slums went with fresh hope to the Dominions of the fast-expanding British Empire. Jackson, the thieves' missionary, was personally responsible for making nearly two hundred of them fit to go.

'There was joy in thievedom,' as he expressed it, that at last a door of opportunity was opening, and a way of escape from the misery of lives spent between spells in prison and scraping a dishonest livelihood out of it. He went to see them off to the New World, and emotions ran high when the time came to say goodbye. One lad clung to him weeping, one of many who had been abandoned by his parents when a child, and had dragged out a pitiful existence in the streets until he met Jackson. He was the only father the boy had ever known.

A quarter of a century later, Dr. Barnardo was to start rescuing such boys, and William Booth to found the Salvation Army, but in the 1840s the London City Mission

was alone in the field. The liaison between its missionaries
and such men as Lord Ashley, Earl of Shaftesbury, was a
major factor in improving conditions among the victims of
the industrial revolution, rotting in the London slums.

Chapter Four

PHILANTHROPY BECOMES FASHIONABLE

Philanthropy was in the air. What with Charles Dickens writing harrowing novels about life in slums and work-houses, and the Prince Consort himself becoming president of a society for the improvement of conditions for the labouring classes, public attention was being drawn to the regions where poverty reigned. And since some members of the upper classes were known to be actually going to those horrid quarters to see for themselves what was being done to help their inhabitants, it became quite the right thing to do to go there. Ladies in capes and crinolines, accompanied by gentlemen in top hats and long-tailed coats, were to be seen driving up in carriages to grace with their presence special functions arranged for the poor. Lord Ashley, writing up his diary after taking the chair at one such gathering, reported, 'Last night tea party at Jurston Road Ragged School. A wondrous company on the platform! These things are now becoming "fashionable"' he added drily. 'Humanity will soon be considered elegant, genteel ...'

Whatever may have been the motives of those whose names appeared on subscription lists for furthering good causes, the fact that some of their superfluous wealth was being directed towards London's deprived areas worked well for the London City Mission. By the end of its first twenty years it was supporting 330 missionaries with no other income than what came from voluntary contributions. Garden parties and meetings in drawing-rooms to raise funds were organised by public-spirited hostesses, and some of them went further than that – they offered their personal help to the missionaries by teaching in the Ragged Schools, or visiting the bed-ridden. It was due to the vision and enterprise of a London City Missionary, with the support of several such ladies, that a scheme was introduced which was to be adapted far and wide, and in a modified form continues to the present day.

A Mothers' Meeting was started in the vicinity of Berkeley Square. The missionary working in the back streets arranged for about twenty of the women he met in the course of his visitations to meet a few of 'the ladies from the big houses' who were willing to help them. At that preliminary gathering it emerged that most of the slum dwellers knew next to nothing of the rudiments of housewifery – some of them could not even sew. Well, since there were Ragged Schools to teach children to read and write, why not start a weekly meeting to teach mothers the simple art of needlework and follow it up by teaching them to sing hymns, and pray, and learn about Jesus?

It was something quite new. A meeting specially for women, where they could be together and learn to do something useful! The men congregated together in the 'gin palaces' and came back drunk from them as often as not, but where could the women get together except in twos and threes for a gossip on the doorsteps?

The Mothers' Meeting was a huge success. It provided a welcome change for women to get out of their dingy little rooms to sit together for an hour or two in a cheerful atmosphere, with something to show for it at the end. Those with deft fingers were delighted to discover how old garments could be cut down and made over to look as good as new. And it was refreshing to spend the last part of the afternoon listening to words that somehow spoke to the heart. The membership doubled, then doubled again, and when there were 150 names on the register it was decided the meeting must be subdivided. Over 150 women at one time were too many to cope with.

When another meeting of twelve members increased with amazing rapidity to 173 it was evident that the scheme had really got off the ground. A further development was a weekly subscription of two pennies per member which, when judiciously augmented by generous contributions from 'the ladies from the big houses', bought lengths of new material which could be made up into blouses and dresses, clothes for the children, curtains for the windows. Members of Mothers' Meetings began to be distinguished by the improved appearances of themselves, their families and their homes. Mothers' Meetings were started in one after another of the poorer districts of London, with the same results. It was not only the women in the slums who benefited from the scheme, either. Many of 'the ladies from the big houses', whose days had been spent in the imprisoning idleness of affluent Victorianism, now found an outlet for their energies and enterprise which gave purpose to their lives.

But that is another story. The effects of the Mothers' Meetings in the slums was that with the raising of the moral and spiritual standards of the mothers themselves came improvement of conditions in their homes.

Not that the primary concern of the missionaries was the improving of social conditions. Far less was it the introduction of legislation that would put a curb on vice, greatly as that was needed. Anything along that line was beyond them, and not in the terms of their contracts, either. Their main job was to evangelise, and they expected to do it on a one-by-one basis. So when a young missionary broke the unwritten law of his society and went into a public house, he had no other aim in mind but to speak to the sick man he had just seen being helped inside by his wife.

It took him some time to make up his mind to do it. The function of the inn, that time-honoured institution where the traveller finds rest and refreshment, had deteriorated in the city into a place where people merely went to drink intoxicants. They had no other reason for going there. If people saw him, a City missionary, going into a pub, what would they think? He did not like the idea at all, but the realisation that the man probably had not long to live, and would be hopelessly drunk by the evening, spurred him on. It was now or never. So into the huge bar he went, with its sanded floor and all-pervading smell of beer and alcohol, looked round for the man he was seeking, saw him propped up on a stool between two barrels as a sort of improvised armchair, walked across and started talking to him.

The young missionary's appearance and manner, neat and quiet as it was, soon attracted attention. What was he up to, this young stranger who evidently hadn't come in for a drink, but only to have an earnest talk with a sick man? A group began to gather round, and when they heard that the subject under discussion was the relationship of man to his Maker, angry murmurs brought the publican on the scene, who promptly turned the missionary off the premises. So ended his first visit to a public house. It might have been his last, had it not been that a week later the sick man's wife came to him with an urgent request to visit her husband. 'My poor man, master, is very ill, and doesn't know what prayer to say. He wants you to teach him. Please do you come, master...'

The outcome of that visit, and the ones that were made almost daily until the man died three weeks later, was that everybody in the neighbourhood knew that he had died happy. 'He became a Christian in a public house,' they told each other. The missionary was treated with more respect after that, and when the publican himself became ill, the rector of the parish received a hitherto unheard-of request. Would he be so kind as to visit the publican, who was expressing a desire to see him, as he wanted to take Communion? The rector responded promptly and found to his surprise that the man was perfectly clear and sincere about his faith.

This unexpected development led to the rector asking the missionary to visit all the other public houses in the parish. The committee of the Mission then appointed him to Marylebone for six months for the same purpose. It was a sort of trial run, to test out the possibility of deploying other men to visit public houses regularly in various parts of the metropolis.

The young pioneer had a tough time of it. On one occasion

he was forcibly ejected from three public houses in the course of a single afternoon. It was quickly done. The barmen, accustomed to dealing with noisy drunkards, did not hesitate to tackle this ranting preacher in the same way. A grasp of the collar at the back of the neck, a quick push forward, the swing door opened with the foot and a final shove landed the offender in the sunlit street, to the raising of shocked eyebrows on the part of passers-by, who wondered what disgusting behaviour from such a respectable-looking young man could have merited such treatment.

From these humiliating experiences he learned some useful lessons about combining tact with zeal, and how to lead up to his subject by some preliminary and pithy comment on the name of the public house – the Adam and Eve, or The Man With a Load of Mischief (a monkey, a magpie and a young woman), Jacob's Well, The Good Samaritan or The Cat and Fiddle. He developed the art of good-humoured repartee that could turn a conversation to good account, and in spite of opposition from some quarters, he met with surprising friendliness in others. After six months at it, the experiment was voted a success, and as a result other men were allotted to public house and all-night coffee-house visitation.

The task required night work rather than day work, and brought them in contact with areas of vice and crime they had scarcely dreamed existed. Their job was simply to talk to such individuals as were willing to listen to their warnings and admonitions, but they were intelligent men and inevitably they formed opinions as to what ought to be done to curb the evils they encountered. Many of the publicans, they learned, would be glad to close their houses at midnight, when things more often got out of hand, but were afraid of losing custom if they did so. And in the all-night coffee houses, which flourished free of all control, worse things went on than in the most notorious 'gin palaces'. So when, as early as 1854, representatives of the London City Mission were requested to go and see the Home Secretary and the First Commissioner of Police to give evidence about

London's night life, they were in a good position not only
to do so, but also, when asked, to make recommendations
about cleaning things up.

Public houses should be closed by law at midnight, they
suggested, and on Sundays they should be closed for two
hours in the afternoon and at ten p.m. at night. And all the
all-night coffee houses should be licensed, thus bringing
them under police control.

The committee appointed to see into the matter listened
intently to what these simple City evangelists had to say;
agreed that though even tougher measures were desirable,
this was as far as it would be wise to go for the present; duly
reported their findings to Parliament; and that very session a
Bill was passed, and the recommendations made became
law.

*   *   *

The face of London was slowly changing. The restrictions
now imposed by law resulted in quieter streets in the early
hours, and a new industry sprang up to cater for the needs of
night workers – the coffee stall. Coffee stalls in those days
were little more than cupboards on wheels, often run by
enterprising old people out to earn an honest penny, and the
L.C.M. men got a good hearing from the little groups that
gathered around them for a hot drink. If a few burglars and
prostitutes, late travellers and well-to-do revellers mingled
with the all-night cab men, the scavengers, the delivery men
and the railway workers it made no difference, since the
same message applied to all. 'Except a man be born again, he
cannot see the Kingdom of God.' In the levelling conditions
of a dark street fitfully lighted by a gas lamp, a chipped mug
of steaming coffee in the hand, standing among a silent,
heterogeneous group of strangers, the message took on a
quality of realism, and was listened to thoughtfully.

Gradually the Mission was penetrating into areas where
clergymen rarely went. Its original plan had been the
visitation of people in their homes, wherever they might

happen to be. The healthy young man who came from a picturesque village near Salisbury, for instance, found his new location of work in the Kensington Potteries district, vastly different from the sheep-folds and trout streams of Wiltshire. Pig-breeding was the basic industry of the Potteries, where there were said to be more pigs than people, and the smells emanating from the sties, the muck heaps, the drains and the stewed pigs' food defied description. But there were some 800 families living there, and someone had to go to them. In addition to establishing Ragged Schools and Mothers' Meetings, he started a 'Rescue Meeting for Drunkards' with such success that within a couple of years a public house had been turned into a Workmen's Hall, officially opened by the Bishop of London, in which prayer meetings and Bible classes, musical entertainments and lectures were held every evening, until the numbers swelled to such an extent that a new chapel was built for worshippers. 'First congregation of West London Tabernacle made up of reformed characters from Workmen's Hall,' he reported. And so it went on. His work attracted the attention of wealthy philanthropists who were ready to support his enterprises, and one of the halls opened in his district was called Shaftesbury Hall. The noble earl had responded to his appeal for help, and later chaired the public meeting for the purpose of promoting Workmen's Halls in other areas.

Similar things were happening in other parts of London as the City missionaries embarked on their quiet, door-to-door visitation, not only preaching but becoming personally involved in the lives of the people. There were times when it looked as though the patient effort was unavailing, for there were plenty of disappointments and failures to balance the successes. One eminent churchman announced publicly that he was not in favour of evangelism in the slums – that the amount of labour and money spent did not produce sufficient results. But the work continued, and the emergence of little meeting places, of Mothers' Meetings, Ragged Schools and Workmen's Halls were like the silent stirrings of life in a tree that had appeared to be dead. And when London City missionaries were invited to speak about their activities, they always had reports to give of ones and twos, here and there, who had given evidence of a change of heart as the result of coming in living faith to Christ. This was always their primary objective, and it was achieved mainly through visiting in homes.

After some years, however, it became evident to the committee that some men could be reached more effectively at their places of work than in the homes from which they were so often absent. The cab men lining up outside the railway stations to meet the night-trains, for instance, had nothing to do while they were waiting, and it might prove a good opportunity to gain their attention, though they were a rough lot of men and it would take gumption to tackle them on religious matters. The committee therefore advertised for someone to do the work, and to their surprise the advert was answered by a cab man. He had had next to no education, but what he lacked in academic qualifications he more than made up for in practical Christian experience. The other cab men called him 'The Saint' because he carried his religious convictions even to the extent of refusing to work on Sundays. They sneered at him, but they respected him all the same, and once they had got used to the idea of his now being employed as a missionary among them, some began to take what he said seriously. Jesus Christ, he assured them, did not regard them as 'outsiders', even though that is what they defiantly said they were, for although they drove many a worshipper up to the church door on Sundays, they never entered themselves. No one ever invited them to do so. But now, here was Adams, one of themselves, with a convincing message that the Saviour was not only to be found within the walls of churches. He was seeking them right where they were, there on the cab-ranks, ready to forgive their thieving and their deceptions, their drunkenness and their brutalities, and make good men of them.

The outcome of Adams' efforts was that a number of the cab men became practising Christians and like him, stopped working on Sundays. They then began to agitate for an alteration in the law which would enable those who wanted it to take out six-day licences. This was eventually granted – a piece of legislation of which an increasing number took advantage. As for Adams himself, after five years of evangelising his fellow cab men in London he emigrated to join relatives in Australia, from where he sent frequent donations for the support of missionaries to the cab men, while becoming such an influential member of his new community that he was elected mayor of the town.

Specialised work among the cab men soon led to appointing missionaries into other communities of workers – foreign sailors, navvies, railway and omnibus men, bargees. By the year 1885, when the Mission held its jubilee celebrations, it was employing 462 men who were tramping the streets of London with Bibles and pockets full of tracts, fulfilling the instructions they had received – to bring the knowledge of salvation through faith in Christ to those they met, and to do them all the good that was within their power.

The pioneering era was over. If conditions in the poor districts of London fell very far short of those of a century later, they were vastly better than they had been when David Nasmith started the London City Mission in a cottage by the canal at Hoxton fifty years before. In the areas where it seemed there had been almost unallievated crime and misery, light and hope were penetrating, and the L.C.M. was no longer alone. Dr. Barnardo had started his work of rescuing waifs in the alleys, the Salvation Army was boldly proclaiming its message in the streets, independent Christian Medical Missions were being opened here and there in fever-stricken slums. At a different social level, men like Charles Haddon Spurgeon and F.B. Meyer were proclaiming from the housetops, so to speak, the gospel of the grace of God.

It was a period of bright optimism. With a population exceeding that of Paris, Berlin and Moscow combined, the metropolis of the British Empire was the greatest city in the world. High were the hopes of its City Mission, working at its grass roots, of what might be achieved.

Chapter Five

THE TIP OF THE ICEBERG

James Attwell's father, his sleeves rolled up and an apron on, was washing down the horse and cart in preparation for an outing to Battersea Park, and James, his sturdy little legs apart, was watching him. He realised that this was something special. Father was a greengrocer, so he used the cart mainly for the daily visit to Covent Garden to buy vegetables and fruit and flowers, setting off with it empty in the early hours, and returning with it full in time for breakfast. The cart also came in handy when there was a job of furniture removing to be done as a side-line. On this occasion, however, the cart was to be used for pleasure, not business, and the horse, of whom James' father was justly proud and who certainly earned his keep, must look as sleek and shining as possible. He must have an extra scoop of grain in his nosebag, too, for he'd have a heavier load than usual. The cart would be full to overflowing with women and children, all dressed up for Bank Holiday, so there would be no room for the men. They would have to walk. But it wasn't far from World's End, Chelsea, to Battersea Park just across the river, and once they were there they could lie in their shirt sleeves on the grass, caps over their faces, and sleep as long as they liked – or as long as their offspring, eager to be taken for a ride on the roundabouts or to be pushed on the swings, would allow.

The passengers in the cart would be friends from the Mission Hall, of course, and Mr. Jones, the City missionary in charge of it, would be with the party, too. They would all have an exciting time together, even if it rained, though everyone was praying for a finé day. This much James had gathered from his parents, who told him that he'd gone with them last year but was too small to remember it. Now that he was bigger he'd be able to run about and play with the other little boys and girls, though he must be careful not to go on the flower beds, and on no account was he to pick the flowers because it wasn't allowed. But there was plenty of grass and open spaces for races and rounders, and when it came time for dinner the Mission Hall party would sit together on the ground in a circle, say grace, and then have their picnic. After that they'd play more games. It was going to be a very happy day, and so it turned out, remaining in James' memory long after many apparently more important matters had faded.

His early years were bounded by the security of his home and family, with the Mission Hall as the centre to which all outside activities were attached. There they all went on Sundays, there he was duly enrolled as a Sunday School scholar, there his mother went every Thursday afternoon to a special meeting for women and his father every Wednesday evening to a special meeting for men. He learned as he grew older that the Mission Hall was not the only one in the world – there were about 500 other men like 'our Mr. Jones' in the London City Mission. From time to time scraps of conversation reached his ears about their activities. They had to keep very careful records of what they did and how they spent their time, it seemed. So many hours each day visiting, so many conversations on religion held, so many tracts distributed. Every now and then reports were published summarising their united efforts. Over a period of nineteen years, for instance, 65 million visits and calls had been made and conversations held, and in the last six years alone, 20 million. They were cautious about publicising results and did not do so until cases had been tested, so when, in 1906, a list appeared at the end of a book, their modest claims of achievements over twenty-five years could be relied upon.

Even if James had been interested enough to study it,

which he wasn't, he would not have realised the significance of the items listed. It is doubtful whether anyone else at that time was aware of the standards they represented: that Sunday was the day when people should go to church to worship God and not to conduct business, that couples should not live together unless they were married, that children should be taught what was in the Bible. These were accepted customs of a Christian society, and part of the job of the L.C.M. men was to change the minds of those who defiantly flouted these customs. So in the list entitled 'Some of the Results of the Work During the Last Twenty-five Years' were included:

Induced to attend Public Worship	137,702
Shops closed on the Lord's Day	2,408
Families induced to commence Family Prayers	22,815
Children sent to Sunday Schools	146,562
Drunkards reclaimed	55,265
Fallen women restored to their homes or otherwise rescued	8,237

Two other categories included in the list were perhaps the most important from the Mission's point of view; these referred to conversions to Christ (49,038) and backsliders restored (12,061).

Such statistics revealed the keeping of very careful records, but little of the personal experiences that lay behind them, and it was the personal experiences that interested most of the readers of the monthly magazine the Mission produced for the benefit of its supporters. One of the missionaries to the 15,000 men in the coal trade, for instance, took the rise out of the coalie who taunted him with the easiness of his white collar job.

'My job's easy, is it?' he retorted cheerfully. 'All right. Let's change jobs for an hour. I'll load those sacks of coal on the van while you read out a chapter of the Bible to these men. Ready?' and taking off his coat and hat he donned a coalie's overall and cap, handed the man his Bible, and started heaving. By the time the van was partly filled with neatly stacked sacks, the coalies who had gathered round to watch proceedings were murmuring their surprise. The missionary stopped heaving, turned to his challenger, and asked when he was going to start reading aloud from the Bible.

'No, sir, I can't' admitted the man. 'I can't do your work, but I see you can do mine.'

'Yes. I was a coalie myself once.' He grinned at the upraised eyebrows of his listeners, and went on, 'So you see, I'm one of you.' He had no difficulty in obtaining their attention after that, and since he enjoyed a song he took his accordion with him on his next visit. 'I'll sing you a solo,' he said, and sang a hymn with a rousing tune. And so he gathered his congregation. And later, his converts. It was well known that the coal heavers were hard drinkers, and that often the horses pulling the empty carts had to find their own way back to the yards, their drivers having stepped into a pub for a drink – and stayed there. But some of the 55,000 reformed drunkards in the statistics were from among those men.

From time to time in the Mission Hall at World's End James would hear his parents telling each other that numbers were looking up, that there were more people at the evening service the last few Sundays, that the man Mr. Jones had been visiting when he was ill had started attending, and his wife as well. The affairs of the Mission were part of these people's lives, as likely to enter into the conversation at the meal table as the rise in the price of vegetables, whether those apples that seemed to be going off should be sold off cheaply, and that James was growing out of his clothes.

Not that wider interests didn't attract their attention too. All these new inventions! Electric light instead of gas? They've got the telephone – now there's talk of this man Marconi inventing one without any wires at all. Machines, too: they say people will be able to fly in the air one day, and travel under water, too. And as for this Mrs. Pankhurst who says women should be allowed to vote – what is the world coming to?

What went on in the world outside the British Isles was of less interest, except when war broke out in South Africa, and our soldiers were sent to fight the Boers. ('Who *are* the Boers?' 'I'm not quite sure – Dutchmen, I think.') South Africa was a very long way off, of course, but it was our men who had gone there, fighting for Queen and country.

Then, while the Boer war was still dragging on, an inevitable bereavement solemnised the nation. The Queen died.

'The Queen is dead.' For over sixty years she had reigned, monarch of the greatest Empire in the world, the sovereign to whom the Attwells of World's End, Chelsea, along with all the Smiths, Browns and Robinsons of Britain had given their unswerving allegiance. Whatever they may have thought and said about Her Majesty's governments, the Queen was beyond criticism. They put her picture on their mantelpieces, stood proudly to attention when they sang 'God Save the Queen', cheered vociferously when she appeared in public. When she died they mourned her sincerely, wearing black ties and black arm-bands, and subduing their spirits even at parties

But life must go on. 'The Queen is dead. Long live the King.' The nineteenth century was past, and a new era dawning. And after all, it was still the same British Empire, more secure than ever after the Boers had surrendered and the war was over. London was still its great capital, spreading farther and farther afield, swallowing up the countryside with its rows of terraced houses as the ancient city slowly pushed out its inhabitants to make way for the banks and the brokers.

A smiling capital it was, too, with its bands in the parks and its boats on the Thames, its flower sellers and organ-grinders at its street corners, its brightly lit theatres and rollicking music halls, where the elegant and bejewelled occupied the stalls and the boxes, shop assistants surged into the pit, street vendors cheered from the gallery. But one and all stood to attention when the National Anthem was played at the end of each performance, not moving from their places until it was over. Behind the affirmation of loyalty and devotion to the sovereign lay the fervent patriotism of a people proud of their country, their nation, their Empire.

> Rule Britannia! Britannia rules the waves,
> Britons never, never, never shall be slaves.

This song expressed their conviction and their aspiration, and as they entered the first decade of the twentieth century it was on a high tide of national security and pre-eminence, attributed in varying degrees, according to individual faith, to Divine favour. Wars and disasters might strike other nations – Russia fighting Japan, San Francisco destroyed by an earthquake, Italy declaring war on Turkey, constant trouble in the Balkans – but Britain was prosperous and at peace. Outwardly, at any rate.

The same could be said for the London City Mission, and there were times when it made its presence felt in quite picturesque ways. There was the occasion, for instance, when the people of Broxbourne, Herts., were astonished at a colourful procession marching along their streets from the station to the Barclay's mansion at High Leigh, where great marquees had been erected on the lawns and preparations were being made to entertain guests from a dozen and more different countries. Along the street they marched, flying flags and banners – Germans and Swiss, French and Belgians, Danes and Swedes, Norwegians and Finns, Indians and Chinese, Spanish and Portuguese and Italian sailors, all escorted by the particular City missionaries who worked among them. Last of all came a cheerful swarm of Italian vendors from the Soho district, and two or three wagonettes into which were crowded a contingent of *ayahs* from India, saris of a variety of hues fluttering like butterflies' wings. Everything went merrily, with a string orchestra on the terrace, games on the lawns, food in the marquees, photographers everywhere, and at the end of the day a series of short talks, suitably translated into the various languages, before everyone set off for the journey back to the station, each carrying a bunch of flowers from the gardens of High Leigh.

Less spectacular but nearly as large was the invasion of almost a thousand neatly dressed men and women to the Buxton's mansion at Easneye, near Ware. All the London City missionaries had been invited to spend the day there, and to bring their wives with them. What a wonderful time it had been for them in those beautiful surroundings, wandering at will in the wooded grounds, away from the noise and congestion and fogs of London! The missionary in charge of the hall at World's End, Chelsea, talked about it at the prayer meeting a few days later.

There was always something going on when the L.C.M. men were at work. A scavenger had declared that death was the end of it, but couldn't forget the parting words of the missionary, 'but after death, the judgement', as he slammed the door in his face, and after six miserable weeks had turned to Christ for forgiveness.

A Christian man in Caine Street, Vauxhall, had given his coal shed to the missionary to turn it into a little place for meetings.

A porter in Smithfield market had taken home the little magazines the missionary gave him because his wife liked what she read in them, and first she, then he, had become a Christian. Then he had started inviting his workmates home to tell them about Christ, and some of them had been converted too.

Sad things happened, too. There was the missionary who visiting a man dying of a fever, had contracted the disease himself and died within twenty-four hours. Who would take his place? Hundreds of people in his district were left without a messenger of God's love.

At World's End, too, they had their disappointments. Young James Attwell, for instance, had stopped attending Divine worship. The Attwells were very upset about it – 'but what can we do? He's fifteen years old, and earning his own living – can't control these young fellows these days..."

James went his own way for three or four years, but then –

'He's started courting. A very nice steady girl. She'll have a
good influence on him.' And when, at the age of twenty-one,
he got married and started going to church again, the
missionary took courage. Young James was going in the
right direction.

Some time later an evangelistic campaign was organised
in the grounds belonging to Sir Harry Veitch, the local
philanthropist, and James went along to one of the meetings.
The preacher had a hard message to deliver that night. His
text was: 'And whosoever was not found written in the book
of life was cast into the lake of fire.' (Rev. 20:15)

As James listened, it was as though he was hearing it for
the first time. The reality of an eternal destiny, either in
heaven or hell, dawned on him at last. He sat motionless, as
though glued to his seat, until the final hymn was announced
and he found himself looking at the words,

> Is your name written there on the page
> White and fair
> In the book of the kingdom
> Is it there?

Is your name written in the Book . . . ? He knew that it
wasn't, and that he must accept responsibility for its
omission. The gist of all he had heard from his earliest days
in the Primary Sunday School, in the Mission Hall meetings,
impersonal talks with the missionary himself, had been
simple enough. Jesus Christ had died for him that his sins
might be forgiven, and all he had to do was to accept that
sacrifice with gratitude, and ask Jesus to come into his life
and take over. He knew it all, and now the moment had come
when he must decide, one way or the other.

It was all very unsensational, not at all like some of the
dramatic conversions of which the missionaries to the dock-
workers, the public houses, the slums and the doss-houses
could tell. James simply bowed his head while the others
were singing, and asked Jesus to come into his life. Then he
remained behind and had a talk with the City missionary

clinching the matter, and walked home on air. The City missionary walked home on air, too.

The first decade of the twentieth century passed smoothly into history, with scarcely a ruffle in national life, and much to encourage national pride, with the opening of a tunnel right under the Thames from north to south, at Rotherhithe – what a feat of engineering! Even more wonderful, perhaps, was the ocean-going luxury liner, the *Titanic*, greatest ship ever built in British dockyards, and absolutely unsinkable! Millionaires were paying vast sums to travel on her on her maiden voyage across the Atlantic, and all passages in every class were fully booked. The launching of the fabulous vessel made headline news in all the papers as she sailed away.

Then came the unbelievable news, the announcement shouted by all the newsboys and blazoned in enormous letters on the hoardings – the *Titanic* had sunk. She had hit the tip of an iceberg and in a matter of hours had sunk to the bottom of the ocean. When ships answering her SOS arrived on the scene, all that remained were a few life boats of shocked survivors, bobbing on the calm, cold grey waters. The *Titanic*, with 1,572 passengers and crew, had disappeared. '... But we thought she was unsinkable!'

Two years later an Archduke in Europe, of whom the Attwells of World's End, and all the Smiths, Browns and Robinsons of Britain had never heard, was murdered. Then it was reported that the German armies were marching into Belgium. Then the island nation that had felt itself so secure learned that it was at war, and the enemy was Germany, just across the Channel...

It was a shock to everyone – and especially to the committee of the London City Mission, though not for the reasons that might have been expected. It was not so much the threat of war that worried them, but the threat of financial disaster.

Chapter Six

WARS

As everybody knows, it was not the comparatively small ice block appearing above the waters of the Atlantic that wrecked the *Titanic*. Had it been an isolated slab of ice floating on the waves, the iron hull of the great vessel would have smashed through it and pursued her way undisturbed. The strength of the ice-tip lay in what was out of sight underneath it – the iceberg itself.

So with the financial dilemma of the London City Mission in 1914. For some time the committee had realised that funds were diminishing. The older, wealthy supporters were dying off and there were fewer and fewer to take their place. The national crisis merely brought matters to a head. At an emergency meeting held shortly after the outbreak of war, the committee was informed that there was an overdraft of £5,000 at the bank and that things were likely to get worse. Some action must be taken immediately, and the obvious thing to do was to cut the number of working hours of the Mission employees, reducing their salaries by 20 percent. Regretfully, the men were informed.

The response to this decision was heart-warming. As the news got about, ministers and congregations in various places took action. Four curates in Leyton went to their vicar and asked for the City missionary's salary to be made up out of their own stipends. Individuals surreptitiously gave gifts to their particular missionaries. A vicar in Holloway, to the great embarrassment of the committee, advertised in the local press for support for the missionary attached to his church. He received a reprimand for this – while the kindness of his intention was appreciated, it was quite against the principles of the L.C.M. to appeal for money in this way. They preferred to make their needs known in prayer to God and requests to their supporters, rather than in appeals to the general public. Prayer meetings were held, and gradually the situation righted itself. Within two or three months the missionaries' salaries were cut by only ten per cent, and a short time later they reverted to normal. Nevertheless, finances were at a low ebb throughout the period of the First World War, for attention was being focused increasingly on the needs of 'the Tommies in the trenches'.

Patriotism was running high. 'In the struggle into which England has entered, the Jews of this land will stand shoulder to shoulder with their fellow citizens,' asserted the Jewish Chronicle stoutly. 'Every sacrifice that loyalty and affection demand will be made, and made readily.' When the King appointed a special Sunday to be set apart as a day of national prayer, intercession and thanksgiving, the churches were full as people flocked to demonstrate, if not their faith in God, at any rate their devotion to their country.

The crime rate fell, too. 'The professional criminal has gone to serve his country,' observed one legal man with wry humour. As for the public houses, with fewer customers and lower returns, the trade was suffering. This was attributed by the publicans to the spread of education, the increase of low-priced entertainments and to government restrictions. Whatever may have been the reason for this falling off in the drinking habit (which proved to be very short-lived) it made the visitation of public houses by the City missionaries even more difficult than usual. By this time there were two dozen men appointed to the work. By and large they had been tolerated good-humouredly by the men behind the bar, many of whom had found the missionary to be a reliable confidant. But now, this attitude changed. Business was bad, and the appearance of a known teetotaller who had come to 'talk religion' was infuriating. It was made very plain to them that they were not welcome, and the time came when the committee decided to appoint the public-house missionaries to other spheres.

Their position was hard enough anyway. With patriotism at white heat, the mere sight of an able-bodied man in civilian garb was liable to provoke sneering remarks about the white feather and cowards who slunk at home while others fought their battles. 'Why aren't you at the front?' was a frequent question hurled at them. It was a pleasant surprise occasionally to hear themselves defended from unexpected quarters. 'At the front? He's always there, and what's more he puts up a good fight!' In one of the public houses in the district made famous by Jack the Ripper, it was some of the prostitutes themselves who stood up for the missionary when he was insulted.

The report submitted by this particular missionary actually highlighted something more sinister than the verbal attack which he had encountered. The iniquitous traffic of young girls to brothels on the continent in the latter half of the nineteenth century had been exposed by the courageous action of a Salvation Army leader and the editor of a secular newspaper, forcing the government to introduce legislation designed to put a stop to it. Those who for one reason or another frequented some of the East End public houses knew, however, that legislation was not proving completely successful.

'In spite of the White Slave Act, human bloodhounds were there,' wrote the missionary. The men who secretly engaged in this evil traffic were usually too old to be called up for military service themselves, and were glad of an opportunity to jibe at those whose presence and words were a rebuke to their iniquity. 'One such openly insulted me, but I held on by the grace of God ...' the missionary continued. It required as much moral courage to face such experiences day after day as to enlist in the forces.

Some of the younger L.C.M. men felt it their duty to join up, but the majority remained in civilian life. A number of them were too old to go into the forces, anyway. One of the items on agendas of committee meetings during the war was the retirement age of workers. Several of those who were over seventy-five years of age were interviewed with this in mind, and it was eventually decided that at the age of seventy-two those who felt they should retire should be free to do so.

Another matter that came up for discussion concerned the increase of Sunday amusements. With the opening of cinemas on that day the committee saw the red light, and made a protest to the London County Council, arguing against it. However, arguments in favour of doing so were based very reasonably on the need for soldiers on leave in London to have somewhere to go, and naturally enough won the day. When the war was over the custom had got a firm foothold.

So had the woman worker. Patriotic fervour had taken her into the munition factories to back up the men on the fighting line, and to fill other positions they had left behind to go there. A taste for financial independence made her very reluctant to relinquish her place in the world of commerce for home and hearth when the men returned.

The thin ends of many wedges were inserted into national life during the First World War.

When it was all over and the Armistice was signed at eleven o'clock on the eleventh day of November, 1918, the face of London itself was practically unchanged, but Britain had lost over a million of her young men. As for the London City Mission, its ranks had naturally diminished during the war and afterwards continued to do so. The flower of the nation's manhood had perished, and the effects of that loss were felt everywhere. The remaining missionaries themselves were constantly on the lookout for suitable young men to join their ranks. That is how it came about that one of them, having had his eye on James Attwell for some time, finally approached him with the suggestion.

'We're needing men like you in the Mission, James,' was the gist of what he said. 'You've got the right sort of qualifications and experience. You get on well with people, you're the leader of the boys' class, assistant superintendent of the Band of Hope, speak at our open-air meetings, give out tracts, talk to individuals. We need men like you. It's not

a spectacular work like going to the ends of the earth as a
foreign missionary, with a fanfare of valedictory meetings to
send you off. Just going from door to door in your own city,
talking to people one by one, introducing them as best you
can to Jesus Christ ... But it's a fine life.' A sudden glow of
enthusiasm spread over the speaker's face. 'You've been
connected with our Mission Halls all your life. Has God
been preparing you to join us as a full-time worker? It's now
or never. The age limit for joining the Mission is thirty-four –
and you're that already. Think about it. Pray about it. Talk
about it with your wife ...'

So James went home, thought about it, and remembered
something. It was a hymn he had often sung when he was
younger and it had inspired him then.

> There's a work for Jesus,
> Ready at your hand.
> 'Tis a work the Master
> Just for you hath planned.
> Haste to do His bidding,
> Yield Him service true,
> There's a work for Jesus
> None but you can do.

It had inspired him then – it challenged him now. He had a
wife and three children to support, and if he left his well-
paid, steady job in the shop on the Portobello Road to join
the London City Mission, his income would drop to about
one third of what he was drawing now. Several weeks passed
before he and his wife, having talked and prayed it through,
decided to take the plunge.

'Trust in the Lord with all thine heart, and lean not to
thine own understanding,' they reminded themselves as they
moved from North Kensington into the dirty, dreary
neighbourhood of Blackfriars, where most of the men were
unemployed, and the women had a hard time of it, making
do with the loaf of bread, the bag of rice, and the couple of
shillings their husbands had queued up to receive, after the

Relieving Officer had been round to see that they had nothing they could sell.

The Attwells could not do much to help them, beyond slipping a quarter of a pound of tea into the hands of grateful housewives every now and then. But their very presence made a difference, with the two Attwell boys backing up their father's preaching by cheerfully playing the organ and gathering the local kids together to form a club, Mrs. Attwell being always ready to lend a listening ear and pour a cup of tea for a visitor. Things began to look up at the Library Street Mission, with one and then another being added to the little congregation – an old man with a flowing beard who rubbed himself over with paraffin to ease his rheumatism, his friend who lived on the floor below became a soloist at the meetings, the blind woman who liked to sit by one of the Attwell boys because they explained to her what she couldn't see.

It was, as James had been warned, all very unspectacular. When he announced that there would be a prayer meeting on Tuesday evening, one woman turned up. 'We'd better go home,' she said. 'Seems no one else is coming.' But James thought that two were enough to make a prayer meeting, because Jesus had said that where even two were gathered in His name, He was there. So the two of them sang a hymn, then James gave the talk he had prepared, then they prayed and then they went home.

'We had a good meeting last week, didn't we, Mrs. Moriarty?' he asked, announcing the prayer meeting again at the Sunday service. Next time six people turned up.

And so James Attwell got started. There was nothing exceptional about his methods. It was just the way most of the L.C.M. men set about it when they were put in charge of a hall. Their home was 'open house', and no one hesitated to knock at the front door any time of the day, and often night, too, when they wanted help. It required the whole-hearted support of their wives, of course. The selection committee of the Mission realised that. 'How does your wife feel about it?' was one of the first questions an applicant was asked. If the

City missionary went home to a wife who resented the sort of work he was doing, he would be unlikely to last long in it.

*   *   *

So the James Attwells continued during the years of uneasy peace between the two World Wars, and the A.R. Thomases, too. A.R. Thomas had been appointed to specialised work among the city police, and it was with great trepidation that he entered the canteen for the first time to introduce himself as their missionary. As he moved in amongst those tall, well-built fellows, all of them over six feet, he felt smaller than his medium height, and the reception he received was such as to convince him that he was, in fact, a very little man. Some of the police officers looking down on him seemed rather affronted that anyone should consider they needed a missionary. They were upholders of the law, not the breakers of it, so what was this little chap with a Bible and a bunch of tracts doing amongst them? One man in particular took offence at his presence. However Thomas, who had not expected things to be easy, stood his ground. He was there with the authority of the Commissioner, on the understanding that he could talk to anyone willing to listen to him. So finding a little group of young cadets, who were rather subdued in the presence of their superiors and at least responded politely to his friendly remarks, he eventually opened his Bible and began reading aloud from the book of Romans. That was what he had been told to do – to read aloud from the Bible whenever possible, with suitable comments, and when he came to the words 'There is none righteous, no, not one' he enlarged on them.

The cadets showed little interest, and the man who had expressed his disgust deliberately raised his newspaper before his face and kept it there. He was within earshot, but made it plain he did not wish to listen by rustling the paper every now and then but never lowering it so much as to glance in the direction of the speaker. After a few minutes A.R. Thomas closed the Bible, nodded to the young cadets, said he hoped to see them again, and went off to enter another police canteen.

The attitude of the men gradually changed as he returned regularly. They got used to seeing him, nodded to him when he appeared, exchanged friendly remarks, sometimes stopped for a chat and glanced at the little magazines he left on the table. And the day came when the one who had most openly opposed him dropped into a seat beside him in a quiet corner of the canteen and started talking in an undertone.

He was in trouble.

No, it had nothing to do with his work. There was nothing wrong with his professional life. It was more personal than that. The trouble was in his marriage. It was breaking up.

Thomas listened sympathetically and the officer, seeing he had the full attention of an understanding listener, expanded on the situation and his own difficulties. He spoke frankly, and so did A.R. Thomas. Sin was at the root of the matter, he explained, and he did not hesitate to particularise, but he did it in such a way as somehow gave no offence. He included himself in the universal condemnation that all have sinned, that all need Christ to put them right.

That conversation was the turning-point in the relationship between the tall, resentful police officer and the dogged little London City missionary. It led to the officer's conversion, and the restoration of his home life. It also led to A.R. Thomas being treated with a new respect in the police canteen. He was winning his way, becoming the confidant of others who had burdens on their minds that they could not easily share. He lent them books to read, started little libraries in the police station, became a familiar figure with his pack of books and his determined manner, turning up in all weathers and making careful enquiries as to the whereabouts of anyone who was off sick so that he could go and visit them.

There was nothing exceptional about his methods. It was the way most of the L.C.M. men set about their work when they were appointed to specialised positions among the railwaymen, the taxi-drivers, the G.P.O. workers. During the twenty years following the First World War, there were, on average, 265 City missionaries working round the streets, in the workrooms, in the canteens, each day.

One of them was F.H. Wrintmore. His first appointment was to the lodging houses of the East End, and it was a tough assignment. Poverty and crime had combined to harden the men and the prostitutes who lived in them, and while ready enough to accept any material benefits they could obtain they seemed dead to all desire for a different sort of life. 'It was a pitiable sight to see, on a winter's Sunday afternoon, six or seven hundred homeless men munching sandwiches, drinking mugs of tea, then falling asleep while we told them about abundant life,' he wrote.

There was one man in particular whose cultured voice attracted his attention and his compassion. What had brought this hard-eyed man so low that he was reduced to selling matches at street corners, and scrounging free meals wherever he could get them? It was not easy to get in touch with him, cynical and critical as he was, for his only response to sympathy and any expression of concern was a sneer. It turned out that he had once been a clergyman, in high office. 'His fall was a gradual fading of spiritual vision. His loss of vision began his drift towards worldliness, pleasures of a kind that are not the pleasures of the people of God,' was the way Wrintmore in the language of his day referred to sexual indulgences in night clubs.

'He lost his living, his wife, his home, his friends. He was, he confessed, an ex-jail-bird. He had left his home-town to hide in London but London could not hide him.' He seemed past all feeling and showed neither shame nor remorse. 'Sin had warped both his will and his soul.'

Although his was an extreme case, there were all too many who, from various walks of life, had drifted into a similar state of deadness, and the young City missionary's sensitive spirit was oppressed. He was relieved when he was eventually appointed to a residential district in north London, and started his round of door-to-door visiting among people who lived normal family lives. They were basically as indifferent to the spiritual side of life as the men he had met in the common lodging houses, but when awakened they responded more readily, and had less to fight against in their habits and circumstances. It was far better, Wrintmore soon decided, to save people from ever falling into the degradation of vice than to save them out of it.

Yet even in that ordinary residential area of north London he came across one of the drop-outs of society. A well-educated man from a wealthy family, he was living alone in a disused shop, with no heating other than a filthy stove which emitted more fumes than warmth. His bed was a bundle of rags on the floor, his only companion a friendly but verminous sheepdog. Gambling, drink and an emotional upheaval had proved too much for him. His family, indignant at the disgrace he brought on them, would have no more to do with him.

When he met this man, Wrintmore's heart was touched. He visited him again and again, assured him that there was a new life to be found through faith, helped him materially, prayed for him, prayed with him. And this time there was a response. The day came when he went off with Wrintmore to the public baths in his old clothes and emerged cleaned up, shaved and tidy, wearing a fresh suit, to return to a dilapidated dwelling that had been scrubbed and tidied, ready for him to start his new life.

His family never really forgave him, but he found his friends among the poor. The courtesy and dignity of his early breeding were evident as he took his place in the community of the church. 'To see him stewarding in our Sunday services, to watch his poise and gentlemanly bearing, was to see beyond his present life and away to his early environment . . grace had triumphed, and the bruised life was wholly transfigured by the Holy Spirit.'

This was just one of the cases Wrintmore included in the report which he, along with the other missionaries, submitted annually to headquarters. They worked hard in the slowly changing conditions of the years following the First World War, endeavouring to follow the example of their Master who went about doing good, healing those who were oppressed.

Then came the Second World War.

It started officially for Britain on September 3rd, 1939, but it was not until a year later that the full force of it hit London. There had been the call-up of men of military age, news of air raids here and there, of ships being sunk, of planes being brought down; news of enemy advances in Poland, Denmark, Norway, then in Holland, Luxembourg, Belgium, France; news of some 300,000 British troops trapped on the beaches just across the Channel, the enemy before and the sea behind ... Then came the epic of Dunkirk, when the bulk of the British Expeditionary Force was brought back to the shores of England across a strangely calm Channel, with a screen of low clouds as a covering, to a nation at fever heat with exultation and relief. When Winston Churchill made his famous speech to the nation telling them that Britain and her Empire now stood alone in the world as defenders of justice and liberty against the tyrant, warning them of grim days ahead, they were with him to a man. Hitler proclaiming that he would completely wipe us out? Bah! Let him and his Nazis try invading our island! Like good old Winnie said,

'We will fight them. We will fight them on the beaches, we will fight them in the hedges, we will fight them in the streets, we will fight them in the towns ... and when it's all over and we've won, we shall still be found standing together.'

For the average Londoner it was still mainly a war of words – menacing words, and ringing words, threats and challenges, news and rumours, words to alarm and words to inspire – but words. Trains with their loads of workers continued running on schedule in and out of the metropolis, shops opened as usual.

Then the Blitz started. London was bombed and bombed and bombed again with deadly accuracy as Germany's Luftwaffe went into action. And not only London – Merseyside and Plymouth, Southampton and Birmingham, Coventry ... The battle of Britain was fought in the air. As wave after wave of German bombers crossed the Channel, tiny swarms of Spitfires and Hurricanes like swift flying insects darted up to meet them, zooming up to strike at the great machines, recklessly risking themselves if only they could stop the enemy reaching his target. Their keen-eyed young pilots, some still in their teens, were trained with relentless intensity, and applied themselves with utter dedication to their one objective – to beat the enemy in the air. It was of them that Churchill said, 'Never in the field of human conflict was so much owed by so many to so few.' During the period of the 'flying bombs' in 1944, the London City Mission reported seventeen houses and twenty Mission Halls to be damaged by them in one month.

It came to an end at last, with Hitler committing suicide, the surrender of the Germans and on May 8th, 1945 the official end of the war was declared to be at one minute past midnight. London, battered and disfigured, breathed a deep sigh of relief. No more blackouts, no more air-raid alarms, no more shattered buildings and shattered bodies, no more being in the front. Fighting was still going on far away in the East, of course, where Japan and China had been at it for years, but the Allies were winning now, and the Japanese were slowly being forced back. Anyhow, it was a long, long way from London. Then it all ended very quickly and suddenly and unexpectedly with the use of a new type of weapon that most Londoners had never even heard of – the atom bomb.

It was very drastic, but it ended the war, and now all those people in Japanese internment camps could be released, and our boys in the forces away there in the Far East could come home. London celebrated with flags and bands, as V.J. Day marked the end of the Second World War.

And surely that was the war to end war, wasn't it?

Or wasn't it...?

Chapter Seven

AFTER THE TWO WORLD WARS

The First World War had left the face of London virtually unchanged, but the Second left it so scarred and battered as to render it almost unrecognisable. Only the Thames, like a great artery, flowed through it undisturbed, its tides licking the wounds along its banks where heaps of rubble and jagged cliffs of concrete revealed the ravages of aerial warfare waged over half a decade. Years passed before all the bombed sites were cleared and reconstruction really got under way, with tall utility buildings soaring up to dwarf the dome of St. Paul's and the slender spires of city churches, and to look down impertinently into the gardens of Buckingham Palace.

In the long run the reconstruction turned out to be greatly to the advantage of the poorer classes, as houses and flats (mainly flats) were erected with all the much-vaunted 'mod cons', flush toilets and running water, gas and electricity all laid on, and all behind the privacy of one's own front door.

Free medical attention was laid on, too, with the introduction of the National Health Service. It meant the end of that familiar institution, the family doctor, but it also ended the embarrassment of calling for his help when you and he knew you hadn't paid the bill he'd sent you for his services last time. Pensions for widows and old people, too, and unemployment benefits without the stigma of queuing for the dole. All told, Mr. Macmillan was right when he said 'You've never had it so good'; the older people agreed, although the young ones, who knew nothing about the Depression of the early thirties, took it all for granted. They took for granted their opportunities for the free higher education, that had been beyond the reach of their fathers, too, along with the better paid jobs they could obtain at the end of it. As organisations like the London City Mission discovered, the poverty they still encountered from time to time was usually due more to mismanagement than to a genuine lack of resources.

If welfare work had been their only service to mankind in the metropolis, they could have reduced their ranks to a minimum. But welfare work was not their primary service, and never had been. Man's basic spiritual needs remained unchanged, and improved economic conditions would do very little to meet them.

It is doubtful whether anyone at that time foresaw the extent to which moral and spiritual standards were to decline in the next forty years. The landslide had not yet started, although erosion had set in during the war, with the falling off of Sunday observance and the increased numbers of unmarried mothers, largely due to the presence of so many Allied troops with plenty of money in their pockets, billeted in the country. It was not until 1960 that the 'permissive society' was ushered in with the introduction of the oral contraceptive pill, and the much publicised court case on D.H. Lawrence's novel *Lady Chatterley's Lover*. When the jury at the Old Bailey cleared of obscenity that hitherto banned book, restraint on what was published in books and magazines, what was heard and seen on radio and television, was virtually lifted. Sex swung into the saddle in the sixties, and on into the seventies and eighties, displaying itself in a variety of forms, illicit and perverted, hitherto unmentionable.

Away back in 1945, however, when women had no fear of going out alone after dark, and people did not bother to bolt their doors, when pockets were picked without the victims knowing it, and the word 'mugging' was unknown, the London City Mission committee had no more idea than anyone else how desperately the metropolis would need the sort of men they had in their ranks. They simply knew that men were required, as they always had been, who could talk to others on an equal footing, and were not afraid to warn them that the Day of Judgment would find them on the wrong side of God's law, and without an Advocate unless they put their case in His hands now, before it was too late.

As soon as the war was over, therefore, they started recruiting again. The first applicant to be accepted was an East Ender named Willy Gray. He had been taken to the Mission Hall at Custom House at the age of five, had put his trust in Jesus Christ at the age of twelve, and when asked, on leaving school, what he wanted to be had answered,

'I want to be a missionary, sir.'

'A missionary!' The headmaster had sounded surprised, then asked quizzically, 'What, to preach to wicked people like me?' laughing heartily when the artless William replied, 'Yes, sir.'

But the desire never left him. He was pronounced medically Grade C, and unfit for military service when war broke out, so he worked in a factory instead, where he gained the reputation of being the only religious fellow in the place. He was afraid that his medical record would go against him when he applied for the Mission, but the doctor who examined him said with a shake of the head,

'Can't find anything wrong with you. Bad heart? Not a sign of it. Don't know why they didn't pass you.'

He started work in January 1946, with A.R Thomas, who had the reputation of being very strict, as his trainer. 'If you get past him you'll get past anybody!' he was told. Certainly, there had to be the most meticulous keeping of records, the most careful selection of leaflets to be distributed, the most whole-hearted attention given to even the most unpromising listener. The missionary to the City of London Police kept his young trainee on his toes, but he did it very graciously, and William passed the test. He was appointed to work in a church in Bethnal Green at first and later in Becontree on the border of Essex, then he found himself in charge of a Mission Hall. In all these places his work was among various age groups, including children, and it was somewhat discouraging at times, like the occasion when only one boy arrived for the Bible Class. But William was not deterred. He had not forgotten what it felt like to be a twelve-year-old schoolboy. The hour he spent alone with Vic proved to be satisfyingly fruitful, for it culminated in the two of them kneeling together on the uncomfortable cork matting and Vic asking the Lord Jesus to come into his heart. William lost touch with him some time after that until one day, twenty years later, he received a letter from a curate in Paddock Wood, Kent.

'I want to thank you for ever leading me to the Lord,' he read. It was simply signed 'Vic'.

* * *

James Attwell was beginning to feel his age. It had been heavy going, travelling from West Norwood to his new appointment at the Sunbeam Mission in Thornton Heath every day, often not arriving home until nearly midnight. Waiting around for buses was a wearisome business. He was glad when a house was offered him in Thornton Heath where he could settle for what was to prove the last lap of his career as a London City missionary.

It had been a good life, and as he looked back he knew it had been a fruitful life, too. It was heartening to get news from time to time of those who had been members of the bands and youth groups he had formed over the years in the Mission Halls for which he was responsible, and who were now in Christian service themselves. Youth work had always been a speciality of his, and although he had more striking stories of conversion to tell from among those of older age groups, it was those who had come quietly to Christ in their childhood and teens and gone on in the path of discipleship, who in the main were proving the most effective. So even now, in his sixties, he was always alive to the presence of the young, and quick to respond to their confidences. When Jean Newton, one of a group of girls who had recently

committed their lives to Christ, came to him for a private
talk, he listened sympathetically to what she had to tell him,
and then gave his advice.

Her problem was common enough. There was a young
man whom she knew to be attracted to her, and she liked him
too, she admitted. But he was not a Christian. He wasn't
opposed or anything like that, wouldn't try to stop her being
one, but he himself just did not believe. The question that
was troubling her now was whether it was right to continue
with the friendship or not.

The conversation, as she had half expected, left her in no
doubt. She ought to break it off. 'Be not unequally yoked
together with unbelievers' summed up the principle that was
to be found throughout the Scriptures. 'What fellowship has
light with darkness?' The choice was clear and had to be
made, and Jean, at no small cost to her own affections and
emotions, told young Harris that she couldn't go out with
him any more, and explained why.

Contrary to what might have been expected, young Harris
was not put off! He began to enquire just what it was that
meant so much to her, to bring her to the point of breaking
off the friendship that was becoming quite serious. He had
done nothing to offend her, the difficulty lay entirely in what
he believed – or in what he didn't believe. So what was there
to believe? The outcome of it all was that he discovered for
himself what was meant by the gift of everlasting life, and
accepted it. His friendship with Jean was resumed, and
eventually they married.

By this time he was in the Air Force, where he got to know
another young fellow named Lionel Ball, and invited him
home for the weekend. Together they attended the Sunday
evening service in Sunbeam Hall, and Lionel heard the
Gospel clearly proclaimed for the first time in his life. Then
history repeated itself as he, too, fell in love with one of that
little group of girls and was turned down for the same reason
as young Harris had been. Lionel Ball and Joan Spencer
separated. They did not meet again for two or three years,
but during that time Lionel was converted, thus transform-

A welcome for Ricky Fawcett in a gipsy encampment

In the Smithfield meat market
The City Missionary among the railway workers

Geoff Holland in West End outreach

Home visiting: John Taylor

On the buses
Getting down to business with the young generation

Lionel Ball looking into the eyes of the law

Ted Young at Tilbury Docks
Peter Schaub talking to overseas visitors

Keith Griffiths on a housing estate in Hackney

ing the situation. It was very satisfactory, from Attwell's point of view, that Christian young men were finding their wives in his Mission Hall. What he did not know at the time was that three of those young men were to serve, for longer or shorter periods, in the very City Mission with which he had been associated all his life. Like his contemporary, Charles Newman, his unconscious influence was to extend into the next generation of L.C.M. men.

Charles Newman had been appointed to work in what were then known as 'common lodging houses', south of the Thames, and to the public houses their inmates frequented. It was not an inspiring task, nor a fruitful one, either. Most of the men and women who were loosely categorised as 'down-and-outs' had lost all expectation or even desire for a better way of life, and making out his annual report one year he rather sadly ended,

'Not a successful year ... I can only point to one definite conversion, and it certainly seems a lot of work for one soul, and at that I was only partly responsible.' (The woman had been converted at a Dr. Billy Graham meeting.) All the talks with alcoholics in parks, with hopeless men and women in dreary canteens, by their bedsides when they landed in hospital, all the money paid out for a night's lodging for someone who was 'sleeping rough', all the warm clothing handed on, and the magazines, books, Bibles distributed seemed to have had no effect. But Charles Newman kept on doing it. He prayed for them, and hoped for them, spoke earnestly to them, arranged a day's outing for groups of them once a year, became known in the areas where he worked as 'the tramp lover', did them all the good he could. And there were times when tears came to their eyes as he talked to them. For some, at any rate, his words brought back memories and touched chords that had long been silent.

'You know, most of us chaps are not so tough as we look. I've often wept when I've been in prison, and I try to pray. Go on praying for us, and try to help us', said one rough, dirty man he met in a park. He noticed that it was usually the older men who spoke like that, those who as children before the Second World War had attended church and Sunday School. With the younger men it was different. 'Ignorance of true spiritual things is normal amongst men under about forty years of age, many of whom have never been to church except perhaps in prison chapels.'

It was an older man who one day handed him a sheet of paper when he was visiting in the sick bay at Gordon Road Reception Centre. When he opened it out he was moved by the power of expression revealed.

A Ballad of Gordon Road

I stand disgruntled, tired and weary,
In this street so drab and dreary,
Waiting for the time to come,
That I may enter my London home.

At last it comes and in I go,
Up to a man who wants to know:
Name and age and date of birth,
And, so discreetly, What's your worth?

I enter thru' that hallowed bower
Where I'm instructed, 'take a shower',
And afterwards, my tiredness shed,
I climb the stairs up to my bed.

At nine p.m. Lights Out arrives
And then we settle in our hives.
At seven sharp up in the morning,
Midst grunts and groans and endless yawning,
To wash and shave and clean our boots,
Though we ourselves care not two hoots!

After this at five-to-eight,
We all for breakfast congregate.
The food is fair, the tea not bad,
No finer can be for nothing had.

We then freeze stiff within our frames,
When told to 'Listen for your names,'
And in our personal interest,
'Go, have an X-ray on your chest.'

Then in a gang, all talk and smiles,
We troop away towards St. Giles. (St. Giles
Hospital)

At last we're told, 'You're free to go.'
But what for? Where to? We don't know.
So once again we're Peckham bound,
We speak of that unchanging round
Of sweeping, scrubbing, shining brass.
Each calls himself a stupid ass,
And thinks of what he might have had
If he'd paid heed, when just a lad!

If Charles Newman's influence among the 'down-and-outs' was not always observable, its effect in his own home was much more marked. The door was always open to those who called, for his wife was as warm-hearted as he. Young Roger Bagge as a thirteen-year-old schoolboy was attracted by their dreamy little daughter Margie, and came to the home whenever he wanted to see her – and sometimes when he didn't, for the boy-girl friendship had its ups and downs, and there were times when ardour cooled on both sides. Even then, however, Roger turned up, for his own home was a loveless one, and he knew there would always be a welcome for him at the Newmans'.

Neither he nor anyone else could have foreseen, on the day when Charles Newman led him to faith in Christ, that he, too, would become a London City missionary. One never knows how a teenager will develop.

And who could have realised the potential in the olive-skinned, dark-haired schoolboy who answered the knock at the door of an old-fashioned Victorian house one day in the 1960s. Harris, now appointed by the L.C.M. to Nasmith

Hall, was in the course of his visitation programme, going along the road of tall terraced houses, all with a flight of stone steps leading up to the front door. Adapting his initial remarks to his audience, he announced, 'I'm from the Nasmith Mission Hall, near Southgate Road. Where are you from?'

The bright eyes flashed and the white teeth gleamed. 'I'm from Guyana – say the West Indies,' was the reply.

'I ought not to be talking to you!' said Harris with a disarming grin.

'Why not?'

'Why, your West Indies Cricket Team is giving us such a trouncing . . . !

The doorstep conversation went well after that, ending with an exchange of names and the promise from the lad that he would come along to Nasmith Hall. It was disappointing that he did not turn up as expected and when, after a lapse of about six months, he arrived, Harris did not recognise him.

'I'm Patrick Sookhedoe – surely you remember me!' He seemed quite annoyed that he had been forgotten. But he came regularly then; he was ebullient and rather argumentative at first, but after a time Harris noticed a change and commented on it. 'Oh, yes, I'm trusting the Lord now,' Patrick said. He made no secret of his faith and his father, a Hindu, was very angry when he heard about it. At one time Patrick was prevented from going to the Mission Hall at all, but he maintained contact by writing letters instead, letters with apostolic flavour, full of expressions of faith and exhortations to 'the saints in Hoxton'. Who could have foreseen that fifteen years later that same young enthusiast would be the founder of *In Contact Ministries*, an international team some forty strong, evangelising in the East End of London?

One never knows how a teenager will develop. That was how George Hider felt, and no matter where the Mission appointed him, his predeliction for organising youth activities soon revealed itself. He was almost apologetic about it when he came to write up his annual report one year, since he seemed to have little else to recount. He sometimes felt that he did not live up to the popular image of a London City missionary, who was known to have a special care for the elderly and the oppressed. But he simply could not help it. He was in Mission Hall work for ten years, and everywhere he went it was the same. Youth clubs were formed, stern discipline enforced, and although it took a long time to sink in that when he said No! he meant No! his clubs were so interesting that the youngsters came and stayed, even though there was a Gospel talk right in the middle of the evening.

When, in 1969, he was installed as District Secretary at headquarters on Tower Bridge Road, his new position merely proved a launching pad for more youth work, with the organising of house parties and camps on a wider scale. This led on to another idea. In 1976 the Bermondsey Gospel Mission was handed over to the L.C.M. and Duncan Whyte, the General Secretary, was wondering what use could be made of the property. As he talked it over with Hider, he found their thoughts travelling in the same direction. Whyte thought of the communes that were attracting young people, where they lived together as a family, pooling their resources and motivated by the same ideals. Hider thought of some of the young people he knew who could give a year or two of service after leaving school or college, who were healthy and articulate, able to communicate their faith, ready to serve without any prospect of financial gain or promotion. Why not form them into a team, send them out in twos and threes to help the missionaries in the day centres, with open-air evangelism, youth clubs, door-to-door visiting – and at the same time give them a training that would equip them for effective service for God wherever they might be?

So an old, rambling building in Bermondsey, next door to a pub and opposite a barracks, with juggernauts roaring past day and night, was turned into a hostel with bunk beds, four to a room and only lino on the floor, a lounge with a heterogeneous array of second-hand chairs around a threadbare carpet, and the minimum of modern conveniences. Here lived twenty young men and women for a year, cheerfully studying and praying together in the mornings, and in the afternoons and evenings going off to their various assignments. When they moved on, another group came to take their place. Voluntary Evangelism the scheme was called, and it had come to stay. It was not intended for those who were looking for an easy life, for whom the demands of discipleship which involve self-denial and the shouldering of the cross make no appeal. But, as George Hider knew, whatever might be said about modern youth, there were some, at any rate, who like it tough!

Chapter Eight

CLYDESIDE TO SMITHFIELD

The year 1948 has gone down in international history as the year that saw the re-creation of Israel as a sovereign state, 2,500 years after Nebuchadnezzar carried Zedekiah, its last crowned king, into captivity in Babylon. It also saw the emergence of Communism in the Far East, with the capture of Mukden in Manchuria by the Chinese Communist forces; it saw the assassination of Mahatma Gandhi in New Delhi; and the beginning of the wind-up of the British Empire as the last of the large colonies were granted independence and joined the Commonwealth.

As far as Great Britain was concerned, the nationalisation of the coal industry was now followed by the nationalisation of British railways and electricity, new social security measures came into operation, and bread rationing ceased. 'The winds of change' were already blowing internationally, nationally, and as always, individually.

They blew with surprising velocity in 1948 into the life of James C. Whyte.

James C. Whyte, commonly known as Jimmy, had a well-paid job as an engineer on Clydeside when one Monday morning he received a letter which he opened eagerly enough, but without any realisation of the effect it would have on him. It was from a friend of his who was studying in the newly opened London Bible College – a very small affair in those days, operating in an old-fashioned house opposite Madame Tussaud's on Marylebone Road. The letter contained a pamphlet, and Jimmy glanced at it with a surprise which rapidly quickened into riveted attention. It was about the London City Mission, their methods of door-to-door evangelism, and their need for more men to do this work.

He had never heard of the London City Mission before, but the timing of the arrival of the pamphlet struck him as being very significant. For some time he had been wondering if he was in the right place, whether somehow or other he was missing his real calling, and on the Friday night of the preceding week his prayers had crystallised into an urgent request. 'Lord – if you want me in full-time work for you, please give me a sign,' he had prayed. 'Something definite, so that I'll *know*.' He had wanted something tangible, and here in his hands, less than three days later, was this pamphlet, pointing out that the London City Mission was wanting men with just the sort of experience in personal evangelism that he knew he possessed. This was no coincidence. God was in this.

He applied to the Mission, was accepted, and became one of their workers in September 1948.

After a period of preliminary training he was designated to Erith and put in charge of the Mission Hall there. His fifteen years in this comparatively quiet neighbourhood, with its rows and rows of terraced houses, were happy and fruitful ones. If he had few dramatic conversions to report, he had the satisfaction of seeing the work for which he was responsible well established with young people who, like himself years ago, were poised and ready for full-time service for their Master. The farewell gathering held in the Hall to say goodbye to Mr. and Mrs. Jimmy C. Whyte was a rather tearful occasion.

His next posting was to an entirely different area, in Lambeth. Here his door-to-door visiting was mainly in high-rise flats, involving him in climbing stairway after stone stairway, to encounter again and again that strange new social ailment of the inner city – loneliness. The old tenements with their outside lavatories and their water taps on alternate floors had practically disappeared – and with them the quarrellings and the gossipings that had ensued while waiting with buckets to be emptied down the lavatories and jugs to be filled from the taps. Everybody knew everybody else's business in the tenements, and those who asserted their longing for a bit of peace and quiet by shutting the door of their room could never be sure someone wouldn't stroll along for a chat or an argument or to borrow something, and bang indignantly on finding the entrance blocked.

It was different living in the new, post-war flats, where every convenience of plumbing, heating and lighting was provided inside, and one's neighbours kept themselves to themselves. Jimmy found himself a welcome visitor in many of those flats where people were living alone. One woman at whose door he knocked early in the New Year invited him in, and he had scarcely sat down before she started telling him of her misery.

'I never see the neighbours,' she said. 'I woke up on Christmas morning, just wanting someone to come to the door. I wouldn't have cared who it was – if he'd been the dirtiest tramp in London I'd have taken him in. But guv'nor,' she went on, 'nobody came. Nobody came. In the end do you know what I did? I went to the pub.' She was sobbing by this time. 'It was Christmas day, and I was all alone, and I went to the pub ... I had thirteen pounds in me purse when I went in, and I came out with less than two ... Christmas!'

She wasn't the only one, as Jimmy soon discovered. The young Scot who came and listened when Jimmy was holding an open-air meeting at the corner of the street dissolved into tears when Jimmy spoke to him. He was lonely. He was dead drunk, though it was only midday, and admitted that he had already spent £8 that morning on vodka, whisky, brandy and rum. He was on drugs, too. He was sleeping around on stations, and got his money by yielding his body to homosexuals, then robbing them when they weren't looking. 'I want to be free of it all,' he said, whimpering. 'Can't I come along with you? You can help me ...'

'I'm just going off to speak at a women's meeting,' said Jimmy reluctantly. The young fellow's pitiable condition touched him.

'I don't care what you're going to do,' was the reply. 'I just want to be in some decent company for a change.' So Jimmy took him along, put him in a seat at the back while he was speaking, and finally took him home. 'We'll have to keep him here for the night,' Jimmy whispered to his wife as they looked at their visitor who had slumped into a chair and was now fast asleep. So they fixed him up in the spare room, and the following morning Jimmy took him to a factory, where the foreman promised him a job if he came along on the following Monday.

But he did not turn up on Monday, and Jimmy never saw him again.

It was not the only time that sort of thing happened. If continuing to go about doing good had depended on the apparent success of his efforts, Jimmy might have felt he had ample reason for giving it up, especially in those early months in Lambeth. The newsvendor in his sixties, separated from his wife and children and living with a woman fifteen years his senior in a damp basement flat; the many tramps who he freely declared were 'a perfect nuisance'; the man whose old, disused mattress was so filthy that the dustman had to be bribed to take it away; the Irishwoman whose hard-luck stories tallied ill with her frequent if surreptitious visits to the betting shop – these were only a few of those who seemed without any desire to respond to the practical help he tried to give them. They accepted it, but made no attempt to use it to advantage. As for the message from God that he had to deliver, neither its promises nor its warnings seemed to affect them, except in the case of the tramps who openly ridiculed it. However, Jimmy was not to be put off. Lambeth, he asserted, would prove to be a fruitful field once the fallow ground had been broken up.

When a Scots couple who responded to his message by abstaining from drink accepted the offer of a holiday in the home of a Christian couple in Kent while their own flat was being made habitable, Jimmy found under the sink ninety-three empty beer bottles that had been there for over a year. The transformed home to which the couple returned, with its whitewashed ceiling, freshly papered walls and new lino on the floor, amazed them as much as their own changed manner of life amazed their neighbours. But such cases were few and far between. 'You're wasting your time on people like that.' Jimmy was told by those who witnessed his efforts to alleviate the lot of a mentally sub-normal couple and their family of neglected children. 'They don't take in what you tell them, you'll never get any results from them.'

'That's not the point,' replied Jimmy. 'I must do what I can to help them, for the sake of the children. Anyhow, the Lord didn't go about doing good only to those who responded to Him. He went about doing good. Like He said, our heavenly Father sends the sun and the rain on good and bad alike. So I must go on helping those people if I can.'

But an even tougher assignment than Lambeth was awaiting him. The first inkling of it that he received was at an open-air meeting at Hyde Park Corner where a fellow-missionary told him,

'The Smithfield Market man has resigned, and they're needing another man to take his place,' adding apprehensively, 'hope it won't be me! I shouldn't like to go there. You'd be a better one for that job, Jimmy.' It sounded like a warning.

Smithfield Market. Like everyone else in the L.C.M. Jimmy knew it by reputation. A man's world, if ever there was one. Men's voices heard shouting, singing, swearing, laughing, as the lorryloads of animal carcases were delivered in the early hours of the morning to be distributed to the various stands, carved up and sold to the butchers who came along to load up their vans and speed off again. It had taken the missionary appointed there years to work his way into acceptance among the men, and anyone following him would have to start all over again. He'd stand or fall on his own merits, not on any reputation from the past. So Jimmy knew what he was likely to be let in for when, after one or two preliminary intimations from the L.C.M. headquarters, he received a letter from his area secretary making an appointment on a certain day, 'Meet me under the clock in

Smithfield.' At the time appointed he arrived at the great
domed building with its wide lanes leading off the central
aisle. The District Secretary was waiting for him, ready to
take him up to the manager of the market to be introduced.
It was midday, and the place was empty except for a few
cleaners swilling down the pavements, leaving not a trace of
the blood and the offal and the rubbish that had littered
them a few hours earlier. Jimmy glanced down the lanes as
they passed them, saw the rows of iron grills that separated
each 'shop' from the next, the great hooks hanging above the
carving blocks, then followed the District Secretary up the
stone stairs to the manager's office.

He was to become very familiar with that office in the
years to come, drink many a cup of tea there, receive many a
request to go and visit this man or that man who was off sick,
or see what he could do to help someone who'd got into a
spot of trouble with the police. On that first visit, however,
he was received with matter-of-fact politeness, given a brief
summary of the running of the market, and introduced to
one or two members of the office staff. It was all over in a
very short time, and he came away feeling vaguely uneasy
about the way the manager had referred to him. He had
called him, not a London City Missionary, but a welfare
worker.

A welfare worker! That was not what he wanted to be.
'Oh, Lord,' he prayed inwardly as he walked past St.
Bartholomew's hospital on his way to the Underground
station at St. Paul's. 'I don't want to be a welfare worker. I'm
here to preach the Gospel!'

And then, like a flash, he received an unexpected answer.
It came silently, but in a way he could not mistake. There
came to his mind words that he had read quite recently in the
book of Nehemiah: '... there came a man to seek the welfare
of the children of Israel.'

There it was, the very word. Welfare. To seek the welfare,
the well-being of others, to make life better for them. It all
came back to that simple commission David Nasmith
outlined for the first London City missionaries over one

hundred years ago, and which had been followed ever since. 'Visit the inhabitants of the district assigned, bring them to the knowledge of salvation through faith in our Lord Jesus Christ, and *do them good by all means in your power*.'

'All right, Lord,' murmured Jimmy. 'I'll do what good I can for the men in Smithfield market.' He knew it would not be along the lines he had been accustomed to, like trimming the hair of a sick old man, or putting bolts and locks on the doors and windows of old ladies' flats, or collecting prescriptions for invalids. The men who worked at Smithfield needed no such help. He'd have to get to know them first, and he soon discovered they had little time and even less inclination to stop and talk to him. He'd have to get started the only way he knew.

'I'm the City missionary for Smithfield – come to give you a piece of our literature,' he would say, holding out the magazine, *The Messenger*, to one man after another as he walked along the lanes where the porters were bringing along trolleys of carcases and the carvers were cutting them up. The reception he got was almost invariably brusque, often peppered with obscenities, sometimes blasphemies, and would have crushed a weaker man. But Jimmy just grinned and retorted,

'That sort of language makes me feel I'm back on Clydeside! Different accent, that's all!' Then, when he got to know them better, he said sometimes,

'I'll bet you don't talk like that when you get home!'

No, most of them admitted, they didn't. They had too much respect for their wives and families. It was just in the Market they let themselves go. But after a time Jimmy noticed that they curbed their language when he was around, although they did not cease to jeer at him.

'How many converts have you made, Jimmy?' asked one.

'I'm not here to make converts,' replied Jimmy with spirit. 'I'm only here to point the way to heaven. It's up to you then. The trouble with you men is that you haven't got the guts to stand alone,' he went on. 'You all go along with the crowd, even when you know you're on the wrong road. Like Jesus said, "The road to destruction is broad, and many go down it. The road to life is narrow, and there are only a few who find it." It takes guts to go the narrow road!'

'Aw, get along with you, Jimmy, you old Bible thumper! I've got work to do – not like you, nothing better to do than go around talking. Get out!' And Jimmy walked on cheerfully. He knew when it was time to go, when he had said enough, who was likely to accept a *Messenger* and who was not – and who should be avoided altogether.'

Like that big fellow who had threatened him with a knife.

Jimmy had approached him with his usual 'I'm the City missionary here – will you accept a copy of our *Messenger*?' and the reaction had been so violent that he backed away in alarm. The big fellow grasped his fifteen-inch knife, pointed it towards him, and advancing with a fluent flow of profane embellishments told him to get out and never come near him again. Jimmy gave his stand a wide berth after that, which probably explains why he had not noticed the man's absence from the Market. It was not until Little Alfie, the scalesman, approached him one day to ask if he'd heard that 'the big fellow' was ill, that he knew anything about it.

'Been away for several weeks. I thought perhaps you'd go and visit him, and find out how he is.' By this time Jimmy was known in the Market for his sick visiting, so the suggestion was a reasonable one, and he agreed to go, though not without a feeling of apprehension. When he arrived at the front door of the house in north London and rang the bell he wondered what sort of a reception he would get. As it happened 'the big fellow' himself answered the bell, and when he saw who it was standing there he was so taken aback he was speechless for a few moments.

'What do you want?' he asked, when he had recovered himself.

'Oh, I heard you'd been ill, and came along to see how you're getting on.'

The man grunted. 'I'm getting on all right.'

'Good. I'm glad to hear it,' said Jimmy, smiling. 'Little Alfie'll be glad, too. It was he who told me about you.' He paused a moment, wondering how he could keep this rather one-sided conversation going. 'I do hope you continue to make good progress – that you'll soon be back in the Market...' There seemed nothing else to say, so he stood there, waiting for the other to make the next move. The man hesitated, then stood back and opened the door wider.

'Want to come in?' he said gruffly. Jimmy entered.

'Want a cup of tea?' asked the big fellow, leading the way into the kitchen. He put the kettle on, then turned to Jimmy and said,

'You can call me Fred.'

'Thanks, Fred. My name's Jimmy – Jimmy Whyte. The fellows sometimes call me Jock, though. Guess my accent gives me away...' That was about the last thing he said for two hours, for Fred, after making the tea, sat down at the kitchen table and started talking. Jimmy would have been hard put to it to recount what he talked about – his illness, what the doctor said, his family, trade, the Market ... It did not matter to Jimmy. The barriers were breaking down, and when at last he got up saying that he must be going and held out his hand, Fred grasped it in his own two huge fists and said,

'Thank you for coming, Jimmy. I've enjoyed our chat. Please come again.' So Jimmy went again, two or three times, and when eventually Fred returned to Smithfield his enthusiasm was almost embarrassing. Spotting Jimmy walking along his lane, he threw his arm round his shoulders and shouted to his work-mates,

'Here, you bunch of so-and-so's,' (His language was as lurid as ever) 'When I was ill not one of you came to see me – not even the manager. Only the missionary. Now if any of you has got anything to say to him,' and he glanced round threateningly, 'He can say it to me first. Got that?' He handled his knife with one hand and hugged Jimmy with the other. 'He's my friend – see?'

Being Jimmy's friend did not have any very evident effect on Big Fred's theology – at least, so Jimmy would have admitted, until one day he found himself grasped by the arm and heard Big Fred's voice, somewhat lower than usual, saying,

'Come along, Jock, we're going to have a cup of coffee.' Rather surprised, he allowed himself to be ushered into The Cock Tavern, and over the coffee cups Fred started talking.

'Last night something strange happened. I found myself thinking about God.' Then, seeing the look of incredulity on Jimmy's face, he held up his hand, and using the Smithfield expression for telling the truth said, 'Straight up, sir!' Jimmy nodded silently and Fred continued.

'You know us men, we has to go to bed early to be up in time in the morning. Well, last night my daughter came in to kiss me goodnight, like she always does, and tuck me in, and I said to her, "Goodnight, darling. God bless you." And after she'd gone out and turned off the light, I thought to myself, that I didn't believe in God, and yet I'd said God bless you. And Jimmy – I started thinking about God... thinking about God . . .'

He looked across the table with eyes that looked bewildered, as though seeking something he could not understand. If he didn't believe, why think about God?

It was all very unspectacular and undramatic, that twenty minutes' talk over coffee in the Tavern, and so was the conversation held one Friday morning some time later, when the two of them met accidentally in the Market.

'How's your wife, Fred?' asked Jimmy anxiously. He knew she had been very ill. Fred looked at him, and there were tears in his eyes as he said,

'She's much better, Jimmy.' He reached out his hand and grasping Jimmy's pumped it hard. Then he went on.

'You know, they say there's no one up there,' indicating heaven with his thumb. 'But I said some prayers, Jimmy,' and there was a break in his voice, 'I said some prayers. And she's better. They say there's no one up there, but...' He shook his head slowly, and gripped Jimmy's hand hard.

The lorries rumbled by, the porters shouted, the business of the Market went on around them just as usual, but as the two of them looked into each other's eyes before they parted

Jimmy gave a little gasp, half laugh, half sob, as he murmured,

'There's Someone up there, all right.'

From the point of view of the Market's managerial office, the sick visiting done by the London City missionary came into the category of 'welfare work', but Jimmy was finding it the best means he had of fulfilling his commission to bring men to faith in Christ. And women, too. 'Jimmy, will you visit my fiancée in hospital? one of the young porters asked him, and of course, he went. It was good to be able to write in his report that year, that she had come to Christ.

There were times, however, when a request for help along a different line led eventually to a similar result. Aeroplane Harry, so called because he was keen on flying and piloted his own plane, called him over to his cutter's counter in the Market one day and said,

'You might be able to help us, Jimmy.'

'Help who?'

'Me and my wife. We want a baby.'

Jimmy was on his guard immediately. With sex as a primary topic of conversation and badinage in the Market, he did not want to get trapped into that sort of talk.

'Well, you know how to go about that as well as I do.' He did not want to discuss the matter further, and although he spoke with a grin the other knew what he meant, and said quickly,

'No, I'm serious. We know we'll never have a family of our own. We can't. So we want to adopt a baby, and I thought you might be able to write some letters for us.'

Jimmy did not know what he was letting himself in for when he agreed to make the necessary enquiries. He had no idea how many difficulties there were in the matter of adoption. He soon discovered that there seemed to be far more couples wanting to adopt babies than there were babies to be adopted, and that most adoption societies regarded a man of forty as being too old, anyway.

'Humanly speaking, it's an impossibility,' Jimmy had to tell Harry, but seeing his genuine disappointment and the depression that followed it, he said to him a few days later,

'Harry, with man it's an impossibility – but not with God. All things are possible with Him. I'm going to pray that you and Olive will get a baby, and I'm going to ask some Christian friends of mine to pray for that, too. You may not believe that God can do it, but I believe He can. We'll see.'

A few weeks later Jimmy and his wife were visiting old friends in Herne Bay, and over the meal table the conversation turned to the men in the Market.

'I expect you have some strange requests from them sometimes, don't you, Jimmy?' he was asked.

'I should say I do! What do you think is the latest? One of them wants to adopt a baby, and he's asked me to find him one.'

'No! You're kidding!' his friend exclaimed, fork poised between plate and mouth, his attention suddenly arrested.

'Not kidding at all. It's a fact. Why?'

'Why, just a day or two ago we heard of a Christian woman in Dawlish who's fostering a little eighteen-month-old baby, rejected by his own mother, and who's praying for a loving couple to adopt it.'

'Now *you're* kidding!'

'It's the truth. I can take you round right now to the lady who told us about it, if you like.'

Things moved quickly then, for it transpired that the foster-mother from Dawlish was actually in London that very week. Armed with her name and address Jimmy hurried back to London, phoned her, got in touch with Harry and his wife, made an appointment, and the following Wednesday brought the parties concerned together. As soon as Harry and Olive saw the little boy they were down on the floor playing with him, while he chuckled at them and held out his arms – 'Love at first sight!' exclaimed Jimmy. The foster mother, having questioned them closely for nearly two hours, said she felt convinced they were God's answer to her prayers for the child.

After that, official negotiations were started and they took a long time, but meanwhile Harry and Olive had their

weekends booked. Saturday after Saturday they went by
plane from Biggin Hill to Exeter, then by car to Dawlish, to
see Ian, and it was as the result of those visits that something
else happened. Ian's foster mother persuaded them to
accompany her to the Gospel Hall in which she worshipped.
During the quiet Sunday evenings there Aeroplane Harry's
faith, which had lain dormant since a spiritual experience in
his teens, was renewed, and Olive openly acknowledged her
faith in Jesus Christ as the only Saviour of men. Jimmy's
heart sang when he heard the news, even more than when the
adoption of Ian was finally announced.

That first adoption was followed by another. 'Jimmy, if
you could find us another little boy, we'd be so delighted,'
Aeroplane Harry said to him one day some time later. 'He'd
be company for Ian – and we'd love to have another one!'

'I'll be on the look out,' replied Jimmy, and this time he
had not far to look. Visitation over several years in his
Lambeth district had led to the conversion of Mrs. Riley, a
friendly soul into whose home neighbours wandered freely.
One of these was a young unmarried mother, whose little
boy came in for harsh treatment from the man who now
lived with her. 'Why don't you get Anthony adopted?' his
mother was asked by people who were angry but helpless to
do anything for the child. When he was five years old the
young mother herself had had enough. She approached
Jimmy with the request, 'Can you find a home for Anthony?'

'Yes,' said Jimmy. 'I can. I know the very place.' And very
soon Ian found himself being introduced to a little brother.

Smithfield Market is a tough place, and there are very,
very few of those who work there who take a stand as
disciples of Jesus Christ. But Aeroplane Harry is one of
them.

Chapter Nine

WEST END OUTREACH

Lionel Ball picked his way over the old boxes and rotting vegetables that littered the pavements around Covent Garden, and turned in to the little square where his Mission Hall was situated. Ten minutes at the piano before setting off again to do some visiting in the new block of flats nearby would do more to refresh him than even a cup of tea, though if Mr. Dixie was there he'd get that, too. As he had hoped, Mr. Dixie greeted him, rotund and genial as ever, and without a word, went straight into the little kitchen to put the kettle on.

'Took a cake out of the oven ten minutes ago,' he mumbled. Then, making his way towards the door, added, 'Go and cut you a slice, to see if it's fit to eat.'

Lionel laughed. 'It'll be fit to eat all right. You missed your vocation, Mr. Dixie. Ought to have been a professional producer of high-class gateaux. You'd have made a fortune,' and sitting down at the piano, with his fingers running over the keys, he started to sing.

He was feeling cheerful and music had always been the most natural outlet for his emotions. Away back in his native Wales he had started playing the mouth organ at the age of two and a half, and did it well enough to pick up many a penny from the men who worked in the quarries, before hurrying off to school. He had joined the choir and learned to play the organ in the chapel, not from any religious instinct but merely as a means to satisfy his desire for music in any form. When an old farm labourer, known in the area for his ardent open-air preaching, had laid his hands on

Lionel's head one day and prayed aloud, 'Lord, use this boy's voice in Your service,' he had stood stock still with surprise and embarrassment behind the hedge where the old man had heard him singing. He was only ten years old at the time, but somehow he had never forgotten that old man's prayer. It had stuck in his memory like his mother's words. 'You'll go to London one day, Lionel,' spoken consolingly as he wept with disappointment at not having enough money to join the school outing that would have taken him there.

'You'll go to London one day.' The prophecy had come true, and the prayer had been answered, too, for his playing and singing enlivened all the meetings for which he was responsible – even the Sunday evening services in the Mission Hall in Covent Garden.

Things had been at a low ebb when he had first gone there in 1968, and at his induction Mr. Wrintmore's prayer for widespread evangelism in the district had seemed almost a flight of fancy. The tiny nucleus of regular worshippers amounted to six – four elderly women and Mr. and Mrs. Dixie. They had been earnest and prayerful enough, especially the Dixies, but as a congregation they provided a sharp contrast to the one he and his wife had left in Tottenham, with its flourishing youth organisations and well-attended Sunday and weekday meetings. But this new appointment of his to the West End had included supervision of the London Medical Mission – a misnomer if ever there was one, for the medical side of the work had ceased to exist years ago. He would have changed the name if it had been in his power to do so, but certain obscure legalities prevented it.

As things turned out, it was a misunderstanding due to the name that got things moving.

One day, a short time after his arrival, the telephone rang and a young man's voice at the other end of the line started asking questions about the Mission. 'I'm a medical student at Guy's,' he had announced, 'and I'm a Christian. I saw the name of your mission in the telephone book, and as it's medical I wondered if I could do anything to help. There's another Christian student here who's interested, too.'

Lionel's response had been prompt. 'It's not a medical mission any longer,' he explained. 'But there's no doubt about there being a need for your help. If you could come along and give us your support, help us get some youth work going, do some visiting in the district...' So the two young students spent their Monday evenings going from door to door in the backstreets and tenements that still remained around Covent Garden. With Joan's contacts among the women and housewives in the neighbourhood, the Sunday evening congregation had outgrown the upstairs room into which it had retreated, and been moved back to the lower hall, where it belonged. Several people had quietly put their trust in the Lord, and the singing certainly went with a swing.

So far, so good. Lionel sat reviewing his situation as he munched the piece of cake Mr. Dixie had brought from his home across the square, and decided that he wouldn't want to change places with anyone. He and Joan had accepted the challenge of this work in the West End not without misgivings, but the advent of those two young medical students had been a reassuring evidence of God's plan. He had little idea of the extent of it, or if the turn of events which was to bring them into a work more colourful and exciting than anything they had anticipated. His was already a full life, for his appointment to the West End included visiting the City Police and the West End theatres.

Of the two, he had perhaps dreaded introducing himself to the police more than to the people backstage, where it was moderately easy to gain an entrance and to mingle unobtrusively with the mixed company of scene shifters, electricians, dressers, workmen, artistes and producers, and nervous youngsters waiting for an audition. Some of them were surprisingly open with him, too.

'You seem to enjoy life very much,' he said to a famous actress after a long talk in her dressing room one day, when she had told him about her career, her plays, her home.

'Darling,' she replied, leaning forward and looking him straight in the eyes. 'I don't enjoy life one bit.' Then it came

out, her loneliness after the death of her husband, her family
problems, the heaviness of heart behind the façade of
humour that entranced her audiences. It gave him his
opportunity to speak of the One who can heal the broken-
hearted, and she listened with tears in her eyes.

On the whole, he found the famous artistes more
approachable than those in the artisan class. Alf the night
watchman, for instance, told him in no uncertain terms to
get out of his sight when he first approached him. It took
much patience and many friendly approaches to break down
his resistance, although eventually Alf admitted that he
wasn't much good, that he'd asked God to forgive him, and
had even got a new Bible and was starting to read it. But the
general attitude towards the City missionary was usually
friendly, if indifferent, and he had no hesitation about going
backstage.

To move in amongst the police in their rest rooms and
canteens was another matter. What would be the reaction of
the sturdy, self-possessed upholder of law and order to an
ordinary member of the public invading their privacy?
Without some sort of personal introduction he dreaded
making the initial approach, but when one morning he saw
that the L.C.M. prayer topic for the day was work among the
City police, he knew that the time had come. 'Hundreds of
our supporters will be praying – it's up to me to go and do
what they're praying for,' he said to himself. So summoning
his courage he made his way to Bishopsgate Police Station.
'Oh, Lord, go before me and prepare the way,' he murmured
fervently as he mounted the steps and opened the door.

Inside was an officer who had a photographic memory.
Stored away in its mysterious archives were pictures of an
elderly man with a walrus moustache, neatly dressed, often
carrying a brief-case from which he extracted books and
magazines and pamphlets, and who took a fatherly interest
in young policemen and cadets, exhorting them from time to
time with an open Bible in his hand, visiting any of them who
happened to be off sick or in hospital.

However, on the day when Lionel Ball entered the police

station the officer's mind was occupied with current events, and he looked at Lionel with impersonal interest as he announced that he was a London City missionary, and presented his card. Then, as he read those words 'London City Mission,' memory got to work and extracted those pictures from the archives of the past. He looked at Lionel again, keenly this time, and asked suddenly,

'Have you come to do the same sort of work as that old chap who used to come around here twenty years ago?' 'That old chap' was not the way Lionel would have referred to A.R. Thomas, of whom the younger missionaries stood in some awe, but he knew the sort of work he would have done.

'Yes,' he said simply.

With a single movement the officer swung himself over the reception desk and stood beside him.

'Glad to see you,' he said. 'Come along with me. I'll show you the way round, and introduce you to some of the fellows . . . That old chap did good work.'

'The Lord went before me to that police station,' Lionel told Joan that evening when he got home. 'I went to the right place at the right time and met the right person. He was certainly the answer to our prayers. Couldn't have had a better introduction.'

The answer to their prayers about widespread evangelism was slower in coming, although quite soon after Lionel had been appointed he got a glimpse of unforeseen opportunities hidden in the area.

He heard of a group of hippies who had barricaded themselves, in defiance of the police, into a derelict school building. If the police were not trying very hard to evict them, it was merely because they knew that if they succeeded the hippies would only go and make a nuisance of themselves somewhere else.

Lionel decided to go along and investigate. They would not let him in at first, refusing to open the door, but he stood outside, calling through,

'I'm not from the police. Nothing to do with them. I'm a London City missionary, that's all. Come to see if I can do anything for you.' So after a time they let him in, and he found himself among a heterogeneous assembly of fellows and girls, old suitcases, broken furniture, and piles of dirty bedding scattered willy-nilly in the bare, musty rooms of the decaying building. They had contrived to maintain an electrical supply by diverting an outside cable into the kitchen, so with an electric kettle they had stolen were in a position to offer him a cup of tea.

'How do you get your food?' he enquired after they had chatted for a time.

'Pinch it!' was the laconic reply. 'Supermarkets – stalls at Covent Garden – backs of vans – that sort of thing.'

He refused to be shocked. 'Don't look as though you grow very fat on it,' he remarked quizzically, glancing at their gaunt faces and dishevelled clothes. He felt a pang of compassion as he looked at them. So young, some of them were, just kids who'd taken the wrong turn out of bravado, become outlaws without realising what they were doing, not knowing now how to get back, even if they wanted to. And they looked as though they could do with a good meal.

Then he had an idea. A good meal – he'd give it to them.

'Thanks for the tea,' he said. 'Now I want to give you an invitation. Who'll come to my place for tea and fish and chips? I mean it. Put your hands up, those who'll accept. Who'll come?' They were surprised, but they saw he meant what he said, and he'd told them he had nothing to do with the police. 'O.K. – I'll come,' and twenty-odd hands went up.

Lionel made a rapid mental calculation. 'Give me forty minutes, then come along and we'll be ready for you,' and off he sprinted in the direction of the Dixies' flat.

'Mrs. Dixie, I need your help. Right now! Will you go over to the Mission and lay the table for twenty-four people, and get the boiler on for tea? I've invited some hippies, and they'll be here in half an hour,' and off he went to the fish and chip shop with his order.

An hour later the Mission Hall oozed with the smell of fish and chips and the odour of unwashed clothes and bodies, buzzed with the clatter of plates and mugs and muffled

comments, and finally rang with the sound of a piano and
Lionel's voice singing, then speaking...

'And they listened! What an opportunity!' he told Joan
that evening when he got home. 'But how can we follow it
up? I invited them to the Sunday evening meeting, of course,
but they need something more than that, something geared
to their mentality.'

They prayed, but although there was a steady increase in
numbers attending the Sunday services and women's
meetings, this was mainly the result of door-to-door visiting.
It did not fall into the category of widespread evangelism.

That there was need for evangelism in the streets as well as
in the local dwelling places was all too evident. It was before
Lionel constantly. As he set off again from the Mission Hall
that winter evening, he saw a young fellow slumping limply
against a wall, oblivious to the swarms of people passing by,
the casual labourers moving into the great market where the
lorries bringing fruit and vegetables would soon come
rumbling in from the docks and the country. Lionel knew at
a glance what was the matter with him. 'Drugs,' he muttered
to himself as he walked by. A few steps further on he saw a
girl walking in the direction of Leicester Square. He
recognised her, too. 'On the game,' his mind registered. The
Street Offences Act had swept open prostitution off the
streets in most places, but not round the corners, and in the
cafés and the pubs and the night clubs. Then there were the
young sightseers, teenagers drawn by the lights and the
animation and the alluring excitement, easy prey for the
predatory human vultures who hovered in the background,
ready to pounce on the weak and the foolish.

There were also the victims of the general permissiveness
of the 'swinging sixties'. He was to be introduced to one of
those when he went, in response to a phone call, to visit a girl
of fourteen and a half who had recently been released from a
remand home. The girl herself opened the door and invited
him in.

'Come and meet my mum,' she said. The three of them sat
down, and then he heard what he later described as an

almost unbelievable story. It was briefly told.

At the age of thirteen and a half the girl had been advised by her child care officer to take the contraceptive pill as a safeguard against pregnancy, since she was already co-habiting with a man ten years her senior. Now she had contracted V.D.

'I can't control her – can't do anything with her,' her mother complained and Lionel, as the conversation continued, felt he understood why. She was evidently leading an immoral life herself. He turned to the girl whom he had been asked to visit, and spoke to her of Christ, of His sacrifice for us, His willingness and ability to break the power of sin in our lives. He warned her, too, of the consequences, spiritual and practical, if she continued indulging in illicit sexual enjoyment.

'But I don't see why I should give it up,' she said obstinately. 'It doesn't do anyone any harm. I don't see why I can't believe in Christ and keep on having sex if I want it.'

'Is the truth of the matter, not that you don't understand why you should give it up, but simply that you don't want to?' Lionel asked, and her eyes fell before his stern gaze.

'Yes,' she admitted. 'I suppose that's it really.' The plain truth at any rate brought the argument to an end.

Writing up his annual report for that year, he felt he could not give a true picture of the conditions prevailing in his area in the West End without referring to the openness of vice which he encountered.

'Women parade themselves in the vilest ways imaginable in order to trap men into their lairs. I am accosted as I walk through Soho in daytime and darkness. Groups of men feast their eyes on sordid bookstalls. One young person each week dies of drugs in the Piccadilly area. A night-club owner informed me that he had attended fourteen funerals of young people he had known.'

Nevertheless, his report ended on an optimistic note, referring to a young man whom he had led to Christ. 'I am fully convinced that there is no limit to the places where the Holy Spirit will guide in this coming year, no limit to the people who will hear the saving Gospel of Christ, and respond to His claims,' he concluded.

It was late in December 1970 that he handed in his report. Less than a month later he was answering a telephone call that was to revolutionise the situation in the Mission at Covent Garden.

The telephone call was from a barrister who introduced himself as Sandy Millar. He explained that he and a young colleague had been trying to help the young drug addicts in and around Piccadilly Circus, Leicester Square, and Soho; they realised that to do it effectively they needed suitable premises in the neighbourhood, and were wondering if there was any possibility of using the Medical Mission for the purpose.

Lionel caught his breath. Any possibility of using the Medical Mission to reach these young people drifting to destruction on the streets of the West End!

'This is an answer to prayer,' was the gist of his reply. 'We've been praying for those young people.'

'And we've been praying for premises! Can't we meet to discuss it?' Things happened quickly after that. They met within a week, and were at one about their aims right from the start. They decided to form a team to go out on the streets and fish in the aimless youngsters there by inviting them to come for 'a cup of coffee, a sandwich, and to hear about Jesus'. There should be no disguising their purpose, no hiding of the Name they were eager to proclaim. Leaflets were prepared with little maps indicating the way to the Mission Hall, various young Christians, nurses, secretaries and students, who heard of the project offered their help, and on Thursday March 18th, they started. Off they went in pairs at seven p.m. across the Charing Cross Road into Soho, Leicester Square, and Piccadilly Circus, mingling with the crowds, praying silently, 'Lord, lead us to the right people ... show us whom we should speak to ... make them willing to come back ...'

They found eight that first night – eight youngsters who came in rather diffidently, looking round the clean, bright hall with guarded interest. A number of tables and chairs at one end made it look sufficiently unlike a church but similar to a café to allay their suspicions, and they found it easy to sit with their elbows on the tables, drinking coffee out of mugs and munching sandwiches and talking to people who showed an interest in what they had to say, as well as speaking to them about Jesus as though they knew Him personally, as though He was right there with them. When Lionel started playing a catchy tune on the piano, and Sandy Millar announced that a little meeting was to be held now, which they were all welcome to attend, but anyone wanting to leave was free to do so, no one moved. Who would want to go out into the cold streets from this warmth and friendliness and music? They stayed until ten-thirty p.m., when Lionel intimated it was closing time, but that there would be another Thursday night meeting next week, and in the meantime, if they'd like to come long on Sunday evenings, he'd be delighted to see them.

About twice as many came the following Thursday, and after that the fishing dwindled almost to a halt. Word got about, and before long the hall was filled with about sixty drug addicts and others every Thursday evening.

It was not long before the team began to see their aims being achieved. The first evidence of it was when a young fellow, one of the eight who came that first Thursday evening, said he wanted to become a Christian and be done with the sort of life he was living. A short time later, bright-faced and cleaned up, he boarded a train and they waved him off – he was returning to his home in Yorkshire.

Others followed. Thursday night after Thursday night there were earnest conversations over coffee in the Mission Hall, and at the end of the meetings, after listening to stirring stories of Christ's power in human lives, little groups could be seen bowing together in prayer. There was Mick, who had been in prison, defiantly saying he wanted the coffee and sandwiches, but none of Christ, who hated anyone who crossed him, and particularly the police. He turned up at the meeting one evening with an entirely different expression on his face, and a smile for everyone. He had prayed to Jesus, he said, and the transformation was evident to all – particularly to the police, for he made a point of visiting the local station to 'make it up' with those he had so greatly abused.

Then there was George. He'd been on the streets for years, getting a living who knows how, but having gone along on one or two Thursday evenings, he started attending the Sunday evening services as well. After the third he stayed behind for a talk with Lionel. He wanted to make it plain that he had now put his trust in Christ, and intended to live a straight life. Jock, too. He started off by saying 'Jesus is rubbish', but his mind soon changed on that point. What he saw and heard in the Mission Hall convinced him of the reality of this One whom no one could see, but who did such astonishing things in people's lives when they acknowledged their faults and prayed for forgiveness. And he found it to be true for himself.

And so it went on. 'Tremendous changes have taken place in the lives of people who seemed to be beyond reach' Lionel wrote in his report at the end of that year. 'Hell's Angels who have arrived at our Mission fully intending to disrupt proceedings have been silenced by the Word of God read with power. Alcoholics have thrown away their bottles of drink and returned to pray, leaving the place much more balanced in their walk than when they entered. As I write I am still rejoicing in the fact that only hours ago nearly eighty men gave undivided attention to the Gospel message, knowing full well that Christ alone is their answer.'

But there were disappointments and setbacks, too. There was the nineteen-year-old girl who wandered in, thin, listless, looking nearly twice her age, with whom they had several talks. What they had to tell her about the love and power of Christ Jesus to deliver such as she from the web of vice and misery into which she had sunk was evidently not new – she had heard it as a child. But at the age of fourteen she had run off and married a gipsy, had had three children, two of whom had died, and now she was keeping herself alive by prostitution. She listened wistfully to what was said, and seemed responsive. They looked out for her eagerly the next Thursday, but she did not come – nor on the next. The following week they knew they would never see her again. She had been found dead in a derelict house.

Then there were those who did well for a time but landed in prison again as the result of one slip back into the old ways. Their former records went against them in the courts, in spite of evidence given of recent reformation, and they were sentenced accordingly. Lionel had to add prison visitation to his programme from time to time, and occasionally answer complaints from the local flat dwellers about the type of person being attracted to the neighbourhood by the Mission Hall meetings. One lady asserted that it was the rough-looking fellows and girls who lounged about the streets doing no good that she objected to – not neatly dressed, nicely spoken young men like that one standing at the door to welcome people in to the services. 'He looks as though he might be your brother,' she added.

'Who? Him?' Lionel glanced across at the one she was referring to, chuckled inwardly, but replied quite airily.

'No, he's not my brother. He's just one of the lads who was on the streets, and came in here and got converted.'

It was good to be able to point out that his was not an isolated case, either. There were many others whose appearance and manner of life had changed dramatically for the better after hearing the Gospel and responding to its invitation in the Mission Hall. The reason why more of them weren't to be seen now was that they had returned to normal life, gone back to their homes and their parents, instead of continuing on the slippery path of vagrancy and drug-taking that led to an early death in the back streets of the metropolis. West End Outreach lasted until 1977, when the Covent Garden Market as a centre for the wholesale trade in fruit and vegetables was moved south of the Thames, and the old site was turned into a tourist centre. With the demolition of old properties and their convenient hide-outs the young drug-takers drifted away, scattering who knew where? The day of opportunity among them here had passed. For Lionel it simply meant transferring his activities from one sphere to another. He now had time for visiting the police in their stations and canteens, in response to the Commissioner's unqualified invitation to do so. 'There has never been a greater need for your spiritual ministry among my men than there is today,' he told Lionel.

Chapter Ten

THE WORLD AND HIS WIFE

As a starting point for an exploration of London, Trafalgar Square would be hard to beat. All roads, it seems, lead to or from Trafalgar Square. It is the inevitable tourist attraction to which the world and his wife gravitate to feed the pigeons, take photos of each other standing by one of Landseer's great bronze lions, and generally savour the atmosphere of London's most notable centre.

So to Trafalgar Square Peter Schaub went day after day, week after week, month after month, year after year. He knew the place like the back of his hand, all the roads leading off it, the cafés where he could take someone for a cup of coffee and a chat, and the cafés where he wouldn't if he could. He could tell people the way to anywhere in London, the best buses to travel on to get there and where to board them, whether it would be better to go on the Underground, and how much it would be likely to cost if they decided to go by taxi. He had a fund of useful information which he willingly imparted to the tourist with whom he got into conversation, while making it very evident that his main concern was their ultimate destination.

'Are you a visitor to London?' he would enquire courteously, then hazard a guess with an apparently unerring instinct as to where they came from, no matter how remote a part of the world that might be. Then he would introduce himself,

'I'm a London City missionary,' he would say, enunciating every word slowly and clearly. No one had any difficulty in understanding him. If he spoke with a slightly foreign accent it merely confirmed his Teutonic origin, for Peter had been born and brought up in Westphalia and had fully expected to spend his life in his own country of West Germany. It was while he was taking industrial training that a question was put to him by a boy in a holiday camp in Hamburg – a question which set him thinking, and redirected the course of his earthly existence.

'Are you a *real* Christian?' the boy asked. When Peter admitted that though he had been christened and confirmed he was conscious that something was missing, he gave him a little booklet to read.

The booklet was about death and judgment, about man's sinful nature and his need of God's forgiveness and of a new life within. As Peter read it, he knew that this was the answer to the ill-defined but persistent questioning in his heart. He faced the issue of the righteous judgment of God, and of being eternally expelled from His presence. Then he came to the end and read the words,

'Dear Reader. If God has spoken to you that you need a new life and forgiveness of sins, if you have never received Jesus Christ into your heart, do it now...'

So he did it.

That is how it all started. He was to tell the story innumerable times in the years to come, how the assurance of peace with God had flooded his soul, how the presence of Christ's Spirit in his heart had changed his whole outlook, given him joy, and a purpose in life, and had eventually led him to Trafalgar Square to mingle with the millions of tourists who arrived there every year, and to pass on the message that had been delivered to him.

He had served his apprenticeship, so to speak, in Switzerland, where he went to Beatenburg Bible Institute for two years, and then did three years of voluntary evangelism in Basle with the Midnight Mission there. The workers in the Midnight Mission went out after dark into the courtyards and cafés, the streets and the restaurants to speak about Christ to the travellers and sightseers from many countries who passed through the border town.

If there was one thing more than another that was impressed on those Midnight Mission workers, it was the importance of self-preparation before embarking on their task of street evangelism. It was the main principle on which the leader had built the work. Without the empowering of the Holy Spirit they could accomplish nothing, he constantly reminded them. Evening after evening saw the workers gathered for study of the Bible, and for fervent prayer for God's direction and enabling. Then and only then were they ready to go out into the highways and byways of the city to meet the unknown.

That early training had stood him in good stead when he was seconded by his Mission in Germany to the L.C.M. to take advantage of the opportunities provided in one of the world's most famous tourist centres. As each new day opened up before him it was like facing an uncharted sea, for unlike the men who were going from door to door in a specified district, or visiting the same depots and canteens time and time again, he knew that the vast majority of the people he was to meet would be strangers who would pass out of his life forever. He might have a programme, decide that in addition to Trafalgar Square he would visit Tower Hill on certain days, Oxford Circus on others, but in any case it was unlikely that he would encounter anyone he'd seen before. It was a case of breaking fresh ice every day, making the most of every fleeting opportunity, introducing as quickly as possible the subject of man's estrangement from his Maker, and how the gulf had been bridged. He always carried with him a case of tracts, booklets, Gospels in a variety of languages to give to anyone who showed an interest. After all, faith had been born in him through a short conversation followed by a tract that had shown the way. His own experience quickened his faith that the same thing could happen to others. But the whole procedure was so apparently haphazard, and the opportunities so short-lived, that without the overruling guidance of the only One who knew how to lead him to those whose hearts were prepared, he would just be wasting his time. So he got into the habit of going into St. Martin-in-the-Fields church to sit in a quiet place, to read and to pray to be brought in touch with the right people *this* day, before emerging into the Square.

He rarely had any significant foreknowledge of an unusual opportunity, so on the day when he strolled up to a couple of young Africans who were wandering around the fountains he had no idea that a door for years ahead was opening to him. The young Africans were friendly, glad to meet someone who was willing not only to impart information about the sights of London, but also to discuss matters that were much closer to their hearts. They were theological students, enrolled in a Roman Catholic college, and they were in earnest about their calling. This tall, close-shaven young German was as earnest as they were, they found, though many of the things he said were new to them, especially his assurance of eternal salvation that was based not on his own good works, but on his faith in Christ's promises. They invited him to visit them in their hall of residence, and he went often, getting to know others through them, and with each fresh intake of students finding fresh opportunities to bring men into a personal relationship with the Christ who was no longer dead on a cross, but alive and ready to befriend them. Ten years after that first encounter in Trafalgar Square he was still visiting the hall of residence, and his correspondence slowly swelled until he was receiving personal letters from overseas to the tune of twenty or so each week.

It was perhaps a good thing that all the people who were influenced by the talks they had with him did not write to him afterwards, or he would have been so occupied in replying to them that there would have been no time left to go to Trafalgar Square. He was stopped one day by a West Indian with a beaming smile who hailed him,

'Hello, Peter! How are you?'

Peter asked in a puzzled way, 'Do we know each other?' He had to admit that he had no recollection of having met the man before.

'Yes, you have. I'm from Barbados. You met me in Oxford

Street years ago and told me I needed Jesus, I needed to be converted, and I needed to wash my shirt!'

'Needed to wash your shirt!' Peter stared in astonishment, then as memory slid back over the years his face relaxed into a smile. He remembered having talked to a young West Indian in his usual way and then, on parting, noticing a stain in the fellow's shirt of which he was probably unaware, mentioning that it needed washing.

'I went home and told my wife, and we had a good laugh about it. I needed Jesus, I needed to be converted, and I needed to wash my shirt! But you know, Peter,' continued the man from Barbados, and his voice became serious, 'I never forgot what you told me that day. It stuck with me, and four years later I was converted. I'm serving the Lord now, in Dublin, working among drug addicts...' There were times, however, when Peter was disappointed at not hearing from those with whom he had had more than fleeting associations. Baruch was one of them.

Baruch was a young Israeli from Tel Aviv, who had come to London to study to be a rabbi. He often went to Trafalgar Square in the afternoon, sitting on a bench there for an hour or two before going off for prayer, and it was here that Peter first met him. Baruch was a devout young man, very serious, intent on leading a godly life, and was looking for the Messiah. He was quite responsive to Peter's friendly approaches, willing to listen as well as to argue, but no evidence Peter could produce would convince him that Jesus was the Messiah for whom he was waiting. Their conversations usually led up to this point, and stopped there. Eventually the time came for him to return to Israel, and he promised to write to Peter, but no letter from Baruch ever arrived and Peter, though continuing to pray for him, gave up hope of getting any news.

Then one afternoon, some years later, Peter was in Trafalgar Square, talking to someone, when he noticed a man hurrying down the steps at the opposite corner and running in his direction. He barely had time to recognise who it was before he found himself enveloped in an ecstatic embrace and heard the words,

'Dear brother Peter!'

It was Baruch. He had said 'brother'! That one word told Peter what had happened even before he heard the next sentence, which came ringing out like a royal pronouncement.

'Brother Peter! I have found the Messiah!'

The whole story came out after that – how on his return to Tel Aviv he had found that living in the same house was an elderly Jew who had become a Christian; how they had studied the Scriptures together, comparing Old and New Testaments until one evening it was as though a veil had been taken from his mind and suddenly he saw who Jesus was. His declaration of it had meant the loss of his job and most of his friends.

'But Peter! I've found the Messiah!'

With things like that happening it is not surprising that the L.C.M. should be eager to enlist other men to mingle with the millions of tourists who visit London in the course of a year. In the 1970s Peter Schaub was joined by Valio Syrjala. For Valio, adjusting to life in London was rather more difficult than it had been for Peter the bachelor. Valio was from Finland, was married and had a young family. While he was at Bible College in Helsinki his interest in people of other races had been stimulated by reading missionary magazines about work in Japan. But when he learned of the innumerable opportunities to reach them in London, the conviction grew that this was where he should be: not in Japan, but in London.

Arriving in London, seconded by the Finnish Lutheran Missionary Society, his first task was to learn English. He did not find it easy, and there were times when he wondered if he would be any good at it. He had taken this drastic step of leaving Finland and settling in London, believing God was guiding him, but now he longed for confirmation that he had done the right thing. 'Lord, let me lead one soul to You here... Give me that seal on this calling.' With his limited command of English it seemed a hard thing to ask, and as he struggled with his studies at the language school at Waterloo he wondered how his prayer would be answered. When it happened the significance of the seal was overwhelming, for the one with whom he knelt and who in stumbling words asked Jesus Christ to become his personal Saviour was a Japanese.

Modoo was in the same class as Valio, and was very lonely. When Valio realised this he befriended him and invited him time and time again to enjoy the warmth and hospitality of his home. 'I don't know what I would do without my wife,' he often said. His home was the centre in which the love and joy and peace of his Christian faith was most clearly demonstrated, and Modoo's lonely soul was comforted in it. But Valio visited him also in the hostel where he lived, and it was here that Modoo came to his point of decision.

Valio's influence on Modoo did not stop there. He often talked to him about his own native Finland, with the result that when Modoo decided to go to a Bible College he chose one in Finland. And when eventually he returned to Japan he took back with him a Finnish wife, to stand by him in his witness for Christ in Kyoto. Meanwhile Valio, more fluent in English now, continued meeting and talking to overseas visitors in London – especially those from Japan.

Peter and Valio were not the only men who came from other lands to work as missionaries in London. Simeon Damdar was another. He was born and brought up in Guyana, and as one of a farming family of thirteen, he knew what hard work meant physically, and what it would mean mentally if he intended to get on in the world. So he applied himself to study, and by the time he was twenty-six he had worked his way up into the position of an assistant accountant in Georgetown. He was married, getting established in life, a reliable member of his church, and he went along unsuspectingly to a day conference hoping for a time of spiritual enrichment, enthusiastic singing and cheering fellowship. It was a little disconcerting when the Chinese speaker at the morning meeting gave a stirring talk on the sacrifice involved in missionary work, ending with the challenge to his listeners,

'Are you willing to give your children to be missionaries?' However, at the age of twenty-six Damdar did not have much of an inward tussle to say 'yes' to that, but it was a different matter when, at the afternoon meeting, the speaker touched on something much more immediate and personal.

'Who is willing to give himself to the Lord for full-time service?'

Damdar felt suddenly alarmed. The question seemed to be directed at him, and he caught his breath, like one who has been unexpectedly arrested. He knew that the question was not really put by that man on the platform, but by a much higher authority, and that he had to give an answer. Was he willing to give himself to the Lord for full-time service, or was he not?

It took him longer to answer 'yes' to that question, but in the end he said it, and meant it. That was in 1965.

And nothing happened. No opening presented itself to him for missionary, pastoral, evangelistic work, no inward urge compelled him to move out of his present way of life. The sense of having been apprehended for a work wholly connected with the furtherance of God's Kingdom among men remained, but it seemed to Damdar that he was being told to wait. Where, how and when he was to enter that service would be revealed at the right time.

Time is a great tester of promises. Eleven years passed before Damdar's call came, and by then he was in London, a qualified chartered secretary, working for his firm and at the same time studying, with one more year to go to complete his articleship as a chartered accountant.

Then it was announced in the church which he attended in Hampstead that on the following Sunday evening a missionary meeting would be held. Which missionary society? 'The London City Mission,' he was told. 'They do a lot of good social work among the poorer classes.'

Damdar disapproved. 'They ought to be preaching the Gospel instead,' he asserted, and felt inclined to give the meeting a miss. However, for some reason he could not define, he felt impelled to go, and as he listened to the speaker he found his views changing. The missionary, Mr. B. Hooper, spoke about the visits he paid to the men working in a well-known factory, the opportunities he had to get to know them, learn of their personal difficulties, help them on occasion, and through his friendship gain their attention to the message from God he had to deliver. It dawned on Damdar that winning souls for Christ was not usually achieved by what was called 'sending off Gospel shots and then going away'. It required genuine humanity and compassion, accepting personal inconvenience and even sacrifice. It meant involvement in the lives and circumstances of others. And as he sat quietly listening and thinking, he heard a Voice which he recognised speaking soundlessly in his heart.

'Do you remember that meeting in 1965? Your promise then? This is it.'

Again there was that sense of alarm, a reluctance to respond. 'Oh, Lord, let me complete my accountancy first...' But the reply came with unmistakable authority,

'Do it now.' So at the end of the meeting he had a talk with Mr. Hooper, asking how one could become a London City missionary...

He hoped they wouldn't accept him, hoped they would say among themselves, 'We don't want this coloured fellow.' But they didn't. He hoped he would not pass the medical test. But he did. And so in 1977 he joined the London City Mission.

He was appointed to work in Lewisham, on the main London to Dover road, and among the mixed population there he developed the gift of quick repartee which often turned the tide in his favour. The white boys who attended his youth club were quite friendly until the National Front became active in the neighbourhood. Then, one evening, he saw that the letters N.F. had been carved on one of the chairs on the platform.

Damdar smelt danger. Something must be done promptly. There was a tenseness in the atmosphere, things were quieter than usual. The boys were covertly watching to see how he would react. Quick as a flash he turned from looking at the chair, and with a beaming smiled exclaimed,

'Why, you fellows, I didn't know you backed the same club as me!'

'The same club?' They looked taken aback, puzzled. 'What club?'

'Why, Nottingham Forest, of course! N.F.'

The tension broke with the laughs and chuckles that followed. Football, after all, was much nearer to their hearts than racial prejudice. But when, some time later, someone stole a pound note, he sternly said that the club would be closed unless the culprit came and confessed that he had taken it. No one confessed, and the club boys discovered that Mr. Damdar meant what he said. The club was closed.

It was while he was visiting from door to door in a block of flats that he came face to face with a boy who broke down when he saw him. 'Oh, sir, it was me that took that money,' he sobbed. 'I'm sorry...' The club was reopened, but from Damdar's point of view it had all been worth while. The boy's repentance went deeper than the mere embarrassment caused by an uneasy conscience, and he turned to Christ for forgiveness and a new life.

A quick retort on the doorstep was often required, too. 'No, I can't take your magazine' said one woman, 'I'm a Jehovah's witness.'

'But I'm witnessing for Jehovah!' exclaimed Damdar with a broad smile. 'How come you can't take my magazine?' She invited him in after that, and in the course of a few visits Jehovah's Witnesses lost an adherent but Jesus Christ gained a disciple.

He was alert for opportunities when visiting people in hospital, too.

'How are you?' he asked one big man he noticed lying in bed in the ward to which he had gone.

'Quite all right, thank you, doctor,' was the reply. Damdar, wearing a white jacket, had evidently been mistaken for a member of the medical profession.

'How can you be all right when you're in hospital?' he asked with a grin, and the man responded.

'I've had a heart attack.' Asked how old he was, he said he was fifty-eight.

'My dad died when he was fifty-nine,' said Damdar, sitting down by the bedside and continuing in a chatty way. 'But he was a Christian. He taught me a lot of things before he died, including some Bible verses I've never forgotten. Have you heard this one? "For God so loved the world that He gave His only begotten Son, that whosoever believeth in Him should not perish, but have everlasting life."'

The big man looked at him in amazement. 'Do you know, I was digging in my back garden and the fork struck an iron plaque. I pulled it up and washed it, and those very words were there on it– those very words.'

The conversation in the ward continued for a long time that day.

'My dad told me that I could put my name in that verse,' said Damdar. 'He said I could make it read, "God so loved Simeon Damdar that he gave his only begotten Son, that Simeon Damdar, believing in Him should not perish, but have everlasting life." "Whosoever" means anybody, doesn't it? It means Simeon Damdar and it means – what's your name?'

'Albert.'

'It means Albert. "God so loved Albert that he gave His only begotten Son, that Albert, believing in Him should not perish, but have everlasting life."'

When eventually Damdar left the ward, Albert had put his name there.

From the earliest days of the L.C.M., when the young missionary in Paradise Court discovered an effective fellow-worker in the widow with the teapot, L.C.M. men have had a special respect and affection for the elderly Christian women in the Mission Halls for which they are responsible. Damdar was introduced to one of them when he went to Lewisham.

'Mrs. Off was notorious for her drunkenness and

abusiveness until she stumbled into the Mission Hall one evening, heard the Gospel and was converted,' he was told. 'She's been talking about it ever since, telling everyone how wonderful it is that a holy, righteous God should have taken on a wicked drunk like her.' When she was too infirm to look after herself she was taken into an old people's home, where Damdar visited her regularly and found her as happy as ever.

'The Lord has a purpose for me here,' she asserted, and as Damdar read aloud to her from the Bible, making comments, she noted with satisfaction that several other inmates sidled up to listen, too. But on one occasion when he went she was not in her usual place, and he eventually found her in another room, with only two old women.

'The Lord has a purpose for me here,' she repeated, and Damdar found it to be true, for with that more limited congregation he had a better opportunity to make plain God's way of salvation through simple faith in Jesus Christ. One of the two old women listened avidly. Yes, she wanted to believe in Jesus. What she had just heard had made her so happy. Then and there, in that little room in the old people's home, another soul, so very near to eternity, took the step that assured her of eternal life.

'She was ever so happy after you prayed with her that Sunday,' Mrs. Off told him when next he visited the place. 'Ever so happy. She's gone now. She died on Tuesday.'

'Mrs. Off,' said Damdar solemnly, looking at her. 'God has a purpose for you here, all right! If you hadn't been in this room with her that day, she'd never have heard, would she?'

It was in 1976 that he relinquished his ambition to be a chartered accountant and fulfilled his vow to go into God's full-time service. Eight years later, as he reviewed all that had happened since, the lives he had seen changed, the sense of fulfilment he had experienced in getting involved in the lives of others, he knew that he had chosen the best.

Chapter Eleven

THE DROP-OUTS

From its inception, the London City Mission had been involved with urban problems, and in trying to solve some of them had often found a platform for the proclamation of the Gospel. Times had changed now, and the days when waifs in rags roamed the streets and families lived together in one room in a tenement were over. But a new set of problems had emerged, as the ever-increasing number of patients in the psychiatric wards of hospitals revealed.

As the L.C.M. men went around the streets they found themselves again and again faced with a new malaise of the inner city – loneliness. Lonely children from broken homes, lonely divorcees, lonely old people. An occasional visit lasting less than half an hour did little to alleviate the sense of isolation, and although the presence of a loving, though invisible Saviour might comfort those who had known Him personally for years, there were those who did not know Him at all.

The sound of a sympathetic human voice was desperately needed, the friendly grip of a warm hand, the presence of a human being like themselves to whom they could turn with confidence. Roger Bagge was one of those who set out to provide for the lonely, and the development of Caine Hall in Vauxhall into a Family Centre was the result of his energetic activity and enterprise. Originally a coal shed, but donated to the L.C.M., it became a hive of activity.

'Every weekday we are open from 10.30 to 3.30. We invite you to come and meet others and relax over a cup of tea . . . Why not stay for lunch? Meals are cooked on the premises . . . If you need prayer or would like our help in any problem please do not hesitate to contact us . . . The Centre is designed for all ages to use.'

With an open door during the day, and clubs for youngsters in the evening, it was effectively meeting a social need as well as providing an opportunity for the Christian faith to be communicated. And Caine Hall was not the only L.C.M. hall to be used in this way.

But the down-and-outs had particular needs. In years gone by tramps were often seen trudging along country roads and begging as they went, ill-fitting clothes hanging around them in rags, old boots cracked, uppers coming away from their soles. In the affluent society of the 1970s, however, things were different. The place of the tramp had been taken by those categorised as 'homeless', and the Welfare State paid for bed and breakfast in special 'hotels'. As they emerged each morning, carrying their personal possessions in plastic shopping bags to walk the streets until nightfall, they were not without some money in their pockets – providing, of course, they had not spent the whole of the weekly allowance the State gave them in one wild binge when they received it. Even those who elected to go 'skippering', preferring to sleep out under the arches at Charing Cross, or in the bandstand in Lincolns Inn Fields, or some such place, received a few pounds. And there were plenty of agencies that could provide them with clothes of a sort. Most of them looked just like any rather carelessly dressed man going out to do some shopping.

But they did not feel like other men. They had dropped out of normal society, and had almost lost their sense of identity. 'When you're like this, you feel yourself getting smaller and smaller each day,' one of them explained in a momentary confidence. They moved around in the crowds of people living normal lives as though they were ghosts.

L.C.M. men like Martin Kilby, who worked among them, were swift in their defence. They knew a little of their backgrounds.

'They were pilots in the Second World War, some of them,

just youngsters in their teens and early twenties. They told me they were boys when they first went into action, but after the third time up they were men – or finished. They changed from boyhood to manhood overnight, and lived for only one thing – the battle. They burnt themselves out in those years. When it was all over, they had nothing left. That's why some of them are roaming the streets now. People forget that.' He was glad a Hall could be opened for them three mornings a week, so they could come in and just sit, have a cup of coffee and a couple of sandwiches. And, after all, the message sent from God was for them, as well as everybody else.

There was another class, however, to whom the L.C.M. had appointed no worker for many years. A.J. Lodge had been missionary to prisons from 1908 to 1935, but no one occupied the position now, although the prison population was increasing annually.

Brian Greenaway had been 'president of Hell's Angels'. His loveless childhood, with a stepfather who beat him, had produced a sullen boy whose hot temper, inherited from his mother, had landed him in trouble many a time. Added to that was a propensity for breaking into houses to steal, so what with one thing and another he'd been put into a children's home at the age of twelve, a detention centre at sixteen, and on his twenty-seventh birthday he was in Dartmoor serving his third prison sentence. It was on that day that the prison visitor who had come to see him left a couple of books for him – *The Living Bible* which he had seen advertised, and *Run Baby Run!* of which he had never heard.

He read *Run Baby Run!* first. It was the story of Nicky Cruz, a fellow like himself – cruel, mean, addicted to drugs, sex and violence. Nicky Cruz had been a gang leader in New York while Brian had been a Hell's Angels' president in Portsmouth, but their temperaments and experiences were evidently so similar that Brian was completely absorbed by what he read. He could relate to it all.

Then he came to the part where Nicky prayed, 'O God, if you love me, please come into my life. I'm tired of running away,' and read what happened after that: the amazing change in his character, the deliverance from those evil passions that had ruled him. Brian wondered if that could possibly happen to him.

He turned to *The Living Bible*, opened it at random at the fifteenth chapter of John's Gospel, and to his amazement found himself reading.

'I am the true vine. My father is the gardener. He lops off every branch that doesn't produce and he prunes those branches that bear fruit for even larger crops.'

His mind went back to an experience he had had a year or so previously, when he had been on drugs, and seen a vision with an almost identical message. A figure in white had pointed to a plant on the window-sill: 'If I pinch out the buds at the end of the branches I can make it grow the way I want it to grow. If I leave it, then it will grow wild and there will be no fruit.' He hadn't understood it then, but had been dimly aware that the figure in white was God. 'I've seen God! I've seen God!' he had told his landlady excitedly when he returned home that evening, and she had asked calmly, 'Were you on drugs?' That ended the discussion, and he had forgotten about it until now. But there in the prison cell, the memory returned, and with it an overwhelming sense of God's presence, and of His readiness to forgive. Lying face downwards on the bed, Brian prayed aloud,

'Lord, do for me what you've done for Nicky Cruz!'

And God gave him his request.[1]

The change in him puzzled prisoner and warder alike, and gave rise to opposition too. 'Call yourself a Christian, Greenaway?' would be the taunt when from time to time his quick temper reasserted itself. 'You're nothing but a freak.'

All the same, the change in him was reported even to the Governor, and after two and a half years he was released on parole, on condition that he would stay for five months in a Christian residential centre for drug addicts run by the Coke

[1] *Hell's Angel* by Brian Greenaway (Lion Publishing)

Hole Trust in Andover. It proved to be the stepping-stone without which his faith might have foundered and his life taken an entirely different turn, as he himself realised when living as a L.C.M. missionary in the Isle of Dogs.

'Lord, don't let me have to work under anyone else' he'd prayed. 'I've had enough of being under authority – and give me a tough assignment.' When he was appointed by the London City Mission to the Mission Hall in the Isle of Dogs, he knew his prayer had been answered. With his experience of hard living, it might have been thought that he would have fitted into life in the Isle of Dogs better than those from more sheltered backgrounds, and perhaps he thought so himself. As things turned out, two years of it proved as much as he could stand.

He was married by this time, with a baby girl, and the first thing he noticed when he arrived at the Isle of Dogs was a couple of toddlers playing in the gutter with sharp, jagged-edged broken bottles, while their mothers lounged against a wall, chatting. Broken bottles! Those jagged edges! He'd seen too many of them, used them himself in gang fights, to be ignorant of the injuries they could inflict in a moment, and there were two kids handling them as if they were harmless toys. And their mothers just looking on, indifferent to their danger!

It gave him an unpleasant shock to see the apathy that was to confront him time and again in that area of dying dockland in the East End. The spiritual apathy of those who came to the Mission Hall discouraged him too, and he realised in a new way what those months in the residential centre had meant to him. There he had seen true love in action. His thoughts went again and again to men who, like himself, had turned to God while in prison. He had been fortunate, having been put in touch with the Coke Hole Trust while still there, and he wondered what sort of a person he would have become without it. What of those other fellows, emerging from prison with nowhere to go but back to the very place they'd got into trouble? The thought persisted so that eventually he told the Rev. Duncan Whyte, the General Secretary of the London City Mission, how he was feeling. He simply must do something to help the men coming out of prison.

He left the Isle of Dogs, and was appointed missionary to prisons instead.

He had to make his own way. It was a strange reversal of roles for him to find himself inside prisons as the accredited member of a well-established Christian organisation, and it was not without its embarrassing moments.

'Oh, hello! So you've turned up again, have you?' sneered one warder who recognised him as a former convict. 'What are you in for this time?' Not all the chaplains accepted him, either, but when those who did invited him to tell his story at meetings he had his opportunity. He could speak to the hundreds of men sitting silently before him as one of themselves, and what he had to tell them rang true. Before long he found himself posting letters and parcels of books to individual prisoners at the rate of twelve a day, in addition to keeping in touch with an increasing number of men who, like himself, had met the risen Christ within prison walls and were now trying to live as Christians outside them. His own experiences and struggles, particularly in the Isle of Dogs, had qualified him to help them.

Chapter Twelve

FEAR ON THE DOORSTEP

Things were getting worse: the older men in the L.C.M. were agreed on this. Materially, people were better off than before, but as far as their own work was concerned, it was much harder than when they started.

When William Gray first visited in the flats and houses in his area shortly after the war, doors had been opened to him readily, and he had been invited in without question or suspicion, even though a complete stranger. It was different now. A knock or a ring, as likely as not, would elicit the sound of movement on the other side of the door, followed by silence or the resentful call from within, 'Who is it? What do you want?' And it was virtually impossible to get into some of the blocks of flats at all unless you could identify yourself as a particular friend. It all took much longer than in the old days, when homes were unprotected because there was no fear of vandalism by gangs of boys, or of robbery by men posing as workmen from the Gas or Electricity Boards.

The attitude of people had changed too. It was not that they were more antagonistic, but their attention was more difficult to obtain. As likely as not the TV would be switched on, and the programme continuing with the sound undiminished. And even without that competition there was a barrier of indifference much more resistant than thirty forty years ago - indifference to anything that could not be explained in a material sense, indifference to the consequences of wrong-doing, indifference to that unseen Being, God, indifference to what the Bible contained. People wanted to eat, drink and be as merry as possible, own all the latest gadgets, have longer holidays and draw bigger salaries, since eventually they would die and that would be the end of it. Light-hearted optimists even talked about going to a better world, they hoped! Any suggestion that accounts must be rendered at the end of life's day, that a Judge had to be faced, met with an unbelieving shrug of the shoulders. Who cared, anyway? In such an atmosphere the offer of forgiveness granted to the penitent seemed irrelevant, since no one wanted it. "Scuse me – I want to get the football results – see if I've won the pools!'

Youth work, too, was much harder. Children were no longer sent off to Sunday School, even by parents who were glad to get rid of them for an hour or two, while in clubs they were getting more and more difficult to discipline. 'You deserve a good hiding for behaviour like that!' carried no threat with it, for the youngsters knew the law. Strike a child for however foul an offence and you could be charged with assault and brought before the Bench. 'You wouldn't dare hit me – I'd report you!' Exclusion from the club was in some cases the only form of punishment, and that would probably bring bricks through the window.

The worst areas, probably, were some of the new housing estates, so when Duncan Whyte appointed John Taylor to one in West Croydon, he realised he was giving him a tough assignment. If the local Councillor had had his way, the little Presbyterian Mission Hall on the site would have been turned into a community centre, complete with a bar, bingo and billiards, and that would have been the end of the Christian presence in the neighbourhood. However, the London City Mission took it over instead, and John Taylor and his wife moved in.

There was no door at the bottom of the stairs leading up to the flat, so the local youngsters had quite a lot of fun racing up and banging on the front door. It seemed a good place to go and have a drink, too. The fourteen-year-olds were getting alcohol from the local off-licence without difficulty, Taylor discovered. There was little he could do about that, but he wasn't prepared to allow them to drink right outside his front door.

It was hard to get alongside them. He tried persuasion. 'We'll have a Youth Club, where you can come and play games, have teams, pop music...' They were erratic in their attendance, turning up sometimes, either too early or too late, then staying away altogether. Their behaviour when they came left him exhausted at the end of the evening.

He tried argument, especially when he saw how the teenage boys were stealing cars and motor cycles to go joy-riding till the petrol ran out. 'You'll land yourselves in prison if you go on like this,' and some did. They were all a bit subdued for a short time after one of them actually got killed when he had an accident with the car he had stolen, but it didn't last long.

As for threatening to report them to their parents if he found them drinking, he knew as well as they did how much good that would do. In most cases the parents did not care. Drinking was part of their existence, the indispensable centre around which their social lives revolved, and although they might put on a show of anger if they found their kids were drinking on the sly, they would make very little effort to prevent them.

The Taylors stuck their assignment with all its difficulties for four years. It was doubtful whether they would have lasted that long had it not been for Shirley and Pat.

Shirley and Pat lived next door to each other, and theirs were the second and third houses on whose front doors Taylor knocked when he started his house-to-house visiting. They were both ready to accept the *Messengers* he offered them, listen to his explanation of why he had called, nod thoughtfully at what he said, invite him to come again. Pat had been brought up to go to The Salvation Army, she told him, and when Shirley's husband died before the birth of their second child, she needed all the help and support the Taylors could give her.

Both the women were converted within the year. They were the tiny nucleus of the Sunday evening meetings the

Taylors started in the Mission Hall, the two people on the housing estate whose eyes met theirs with love and confidence, and whose faith encouraged them when things looked grey and lifeless.

In the years that followed a few others joined them, and when Taylor went to see Duncan Whyte to explain how he was feeling, he could tell him that the work, though small, was established. But as far as he himself was concerned, he was exhausted. It was not that he was restless, or was wanting to run away from the difficulties. He simply knew that he was worn down, had no more strength to put into the work.

Duncan Whyte understood. 'You need a change,' he said, 'and you shall have it.' So he was appointed to Clapham Park, to work with a well-established Baptist Church where the staff met regularly together for prayer and planning, where he was the member of a team, and where his home and family were free from harassment.

It provided just the encouragement and renewal that he needed to enter into situations caused now not only by drunkenness but by promiscuity as well. His door-to-door visitation in flats around Clapham Park revealed a larger number of one-parent families than he had ever encountered. Unmarried teenage girls with a baby or two were established on Social Security in council flats which they had obtained without difficulty. Young married couples found themselves low down on the waiting list for housing, and single girls even lower – unless they were pregnant. If they remained unmarried and had a baby they could be sure of accommodation, they were told. They might have to start with a bed-sit, but they'd get a flat eventually. So they settled in with their babies, and their boyfriends could visit them . . .

But some of them were lonely, almost bewildered, like the sixteen-year-old who, with her nine-month-old child, had been left to get on with things as best she could. There was very little furniture in her flat, and only the living-room boasted a bit of carpet. Taylor was glad he was working with a team which included a lady worker. It was the sort of situation that a woman could deal with better than he, and when, from time to time, one and another of those girls started attending church and changed their manner of life, he was glad to have been the first link in the chain that had brought them to Christ.

When it came to the children, however, the problem was the same for everyone. How to help the children? What could be done to get them happily playing games together, how could their activities be directed into healthy channels, what could be done to inspire their ambitions, touch their sympathies? North of the river, in Hackney, Keith Griffiths was encountering the same sort of social problems. And he knew that the children had become a threat to the community.

He had secured a good many windows and put chains and bolts on a good many doors, and listened sympathetically to a good many old women who had confided in him their fears. Forty years ago those women had been sturdily defying the enemy, coming up morning after morning from sleeping in the Underground or the air-raid shelters to view the desolation after another Blitz, to sweep away the rubble and go off to work, eking out their food rations and managing to laugh through it all. But they were old now, and none too steady on their feet, and the journey from the supermarket carrying their groceries home was fraught with alarm.

'They come on you so quickly, from behind, and snatch your bag and run away. And it's getting worse. They'll knock you over and kick you if you try and hang on to what you've got, like they did to that old lady who had to be taken to hospital and had ever so many stitches in her head...'

'What are you up to there?' Keith said once to a couple of boys he found lurking in a doorway. He eyed them suspiciously. 'If ever I find you mugging an old lady I'll give you such a hiding you'll never forget it!'

'You wouldn't dare!'

'If I twisted your arm behind your back and marched you round that corner and walloped you there, no one would know, would they? No one would hear, would they?'

It was the sort of language they understood, and as they looked up at him, with his stern eyes looking at them, his lips tight, they knew he could do it. They didn't know whether he would, but it would be wiser not to chance it. They hung their heads sullenly, and walked away.

But he knew it wasn't really their fault. He longed to draw the minds of these children into something clean and wholesome. He must meet them on their own ground – in front of the screen. And with the introduction of videos he saw a way of doing it.

'Would you like me to bring along a couple of videos to your home?' he enquired. 'I can get some really good ones – they'll make you laugh, but they're interesting, too.' So it was arranged, and he went along one evening with two carefully selected videos, Disney-type, the sort he'd seen children with happier home backgrounds watching entranced.

That evening in August 1983 was one of the saddest he ever remembered. He had joined the London City Mission after doing his national service in Cyprus, and had served in it for a quarter of a century. It was the quarter of a century that had seen the breakdown of morality resulting in one in every three marriages ending in divorce, the passing of legislation permitting homosexuality and abortion, and the blossoming of the permissive society. What Keith Griffiths saw that evening was the effect of it on children.

The videos he took along failed completely to entertain them. Those sort of pictures weren't what they wanted at all. The piquancy, the light-hearted exploits, the exciting adventures, the triumph of good over evil, bored them. They shuffled and they yawned. They had thought he would bring something quite different.

'Why didn't you bring "I Spit On Your Grave"?' they demanded. 'Or that one about the woman being sawn up into little pieces...? That's what we wanted.'

When he got back to his flat that night he just knelt down and wept. He could not really pray, only pour out his sorrow, a sorrow that went deeper than mere disappointment at the failure of his effort.

'Lord,' he said in a broken voice that was almost a groan. 'What can I do? How can I tell those children their minds are being poisoned... that their very souls are being killed... What hope is there for them if their souls are dead...? What can I do?'

If the parents of the children could have seen him, they would have wondered what he was crying about. Religion didn't seem relevant at all to many of them. They were, however, awakened to a real sense of apprehension when they watched the news programmes on their television screens. There had been a lot of talk lately about nuclear disarmament and nuclear war, and violent protests about Cruise missiles being brought to this country. So when, on November 14th, they learned that the first Cruise missiles had actually arrived at the R.A.F. base at Greenham Common they felt uneasy. It was like hearing the siren of a police car, drawing nearer.

There was something significant about the timing of the arrival of the Cruise missiles. That event crystallised the general unease about the future into a tangible fear. Talk was open now about the threat of a nuclear war that could wipe out the entire human race. As one of the L.C.M. men observed,

'In the course of my visitation I am seeing a change in the mood of indifference to fear of tomorrow and despair of the future.'

The time was ripe for the message of hope that the Gospel brings. The widely publicised 'Mission England' and 'Mission to London' in 1984 provided the focal point for its proclamation, and George Hider was seconded to the 'Mission to London' team. The six weeks of meetings in the Queens Park Rangers Stadium was preceded by months of preparation and followed by close contact with individuals who had responded to the evangelist's call to repentance and faith in Christ. It was contact that could be maintained and grow, and lead into homes and communities hitherto closed to the Church. This was just the sort of work that the L.C.M. men were best fitted for. Theirs had always been primarily a one-by-one activity, and would continue to be so. George. Hider summed it up when he wrote:

It was thrilling to be involved in 'Mission to London', and to know that some 28,000 people made a response to the preaching of the Gospel. But we must be honest and admit that although we had wanted 'the whole of London to hear the voice of God', this was not achieved. There were large groups of people who were virtually unreached, among them those belonging to the ethnic minority groups. 'Mission to London' did very little in making contact here. How we need more men of skill and commitment, those who can speak foreign languages and know something of other religions! We have an overseas mission field on our very doorstep. Missionaries who have returned to this country for some reason could be of immense value to us here in cosmopolitan London.

Another huge group, and one which the Church seems to find most difficult to reach, are those who belong to what is known as the working class. It is to this very group that the L.C.M. is especially called to witness, and doors are still open. Our men enter bus garages, railway stations, factories, and workshops, and are able to speak to people who would normally never consider entering a church.

We are committed to this ongoing ministry while the doors remain open. And they are still open. While the opportunity remains, our target and aim must still be that all of London shall hear the Voice of God.

Epilogue

Duncan Whyte drew out a chair for me beside him at the boardroom table, and we sat down together for a brief talk. We had just come up from the hall where the hundred L.C.M. missionaries had gathered for their monthly meeting, and there were one or two questions I wanted to ask him.

The book was nearly finished. It had been a bewildering task to make a selection from the mass of Minutes, books and reports at my disposal, all rich with absorbingly interesting material for the writer's pen – not to speak of what I had gleaned from some of the men I had interviewed and actually seen on the job. But he had been away most of the time I was working on it, so there had been little opportunity to discuss it with him.

'My committee had suggested that as I had been General Secretary for eighteen years I should take a study sabbatical,' he explained. 'Everybody is conscious of the many changes taking place in society – and in the Church. They thought it would be a good thing for me to have time to read and think and try to see what is going on in the cities, and how we should go ahead into the future.

'I've seen some splendid pieces of Christian work in the inner cities. Ministers, clergy, lay members have initiated a host of activities to serve the community. Clubs, community centres, counselling groups, projects for the unemployed, the delinquents, the disabled. You name it, they've done it. And if they had neglected it, the Church would have been failing in its duty. But ...' He paused for a moment, and I urged him to continue.

'But – the Church is not convinced about what else it ought to be doing. It has lost sight of the Great Commission.

By and large, it is failing to make disciples, failing to call people to repentance, failing to bring them to faith in Christ. I could be depressed, but I am not. I see signs of revival and renewal even in the inner city.'

I nodded. Keith Griffiths came to my mind. I knew that he was feeling encouraged by a change of attitude towards the videos he was showing. His audiences sat quietly now, watching them eagerly. Could it be that the tide was turning?

Duncan Whyte continued talking.

'There are new ways of telling "the old old story", and new methods of serving our society. Some of them we have already started, and I have discovered others in the past months. The Mission was founded to be an evangelistic and caring organisation. I am concerned that we keep these two in the right relationship. The proclamation of the gospel must come first. That has always been our primary task. It still is.'

It was time for me to go. I gathered up my papers and rose to my feet. But there was just one more question I wanted to ask him.

'What do you see as the greatest need in the Mission at this time?' His answer was prompt and concise. It had nothing to do with money, or expertise, or methods or equipment.

'What we need is more men,' he said. 'That is our great need. Men of the right calibre. Men with a mission.'

Phyllis Thompson

THE GIDEONS

Almost ninety years ago, two men shared a vision which was to become an exciting international venture. Today, the Gideons distribute one million Bibles every two weeks in 130 countries.

In schools, hospitals and prisons as well as hotels, the Gideons carry out their work with dedication and commitment. Lives have been changed, suicides averted, broken marriages restored, alcoholics and drug addicts converted and cured. The story of this world-famous organisation is enthralling, and vividly captured here by Phyllis Thompson.

Jocelyn Murray

PROCLAIM THE GOOD NEWS

Jocelyn Murray tells the history of the Church Missionary Society, assessing its role and achievements over almost 200 years.

When CMS was founded in 1799, overseas work was a new idea for British Christians. Volunteers were few, money scarce, and the pioneering work abroad fraught with setbacks. But the seeds of the Gospel were sown, missions were developed in Africa, India, China and beyond, and a foundation was gradually laid for the establishment of a worldwide church.